Katie,

Thank you so much for coming to the first Unbound Collective meetup

Kalpana

BEAUTY UNBOUND

Breaking Free and Living Unapologetically

DR. KALPANA SUNDAR

www.drkalpanasundar.com

Some names and identifying details have been changed to protect the privacy of individuals.

ISBN 978-1-7354738-0-2

Author Photograph by
Michele Dobbs John

Cover and Book Design
Mike Murray, pearhouse.com

CONTENTS

DEDICATION

Dedicated to all the women who have ever been doubted, who felt that they had to settle, that they should be grateful for what they have and never ask for anything more.

IN MEMORY OF

In ***memory of Jonas Gerard****, for speaking your truth and revealing your own painful experiences, thus inspiring me to take a hard look at my life. Please visit this amazing artist's website at jonasgerard.com.*

PREFACE

About two years ago, immediately after my divorce, the idea for this book came to me. I was in the middle of getting my life back together after the enormous toll divorce had taken on my life.

I was trying to be a good parent. I was working like crazy to sell my house and keep my businesses running. All while trying to manage the new roles in my life that my ex-husband used to handle for me. I was overwhelmed, to say the least.

Every time I got a piece of my life in order there were a hundred more things that needed my attention. At first, I thought, "This is why people don't get divorced!" But with each area that I took over, something interesting happened. These new tasks and roles weren't a burden; each was a window into my authentic self. I opened up new areas of confidence and understanding. Roles I felt I shouldn't handle because it wasn't my place or that I couldn't manage were the very roles that renewed my confidence. I slowly began to understand how, over the years, I had allowed myself to become bound by everyone else's rules and expectations without once questioning them.

I could finally start to see the life I was meant to live and how different it was from the one I had built. This new life was within my grasp. I just had to have the courage to reach out and seize it. Seizing it meant making bold and purposeful choices to get to where I wanted to be. I wanted joy in my career, in my family, and in my day-to-day experiences. And to achieve all of that, my life needed to be broken down and then rebuilt. As I questioned and reworked everything from my pre-divorced life, I thought I should document the journey in the hopes that my book could help others.

But with all the new roles in my life, I didn't feel I had time to write. Not to mention that writing required being alone for long periods of time. Being alone terrified me. I was already raw and vulnerable from the divorce. So, at first, I hired a ghostwriter. That's what people do, right?

I spent months working with the ghostwriter as they wrote my life's story in a way that would "align with other books in the market" – which is what I was told I needed to do.

When the final manuscript arrived in my inbox, I felt indifferent while reading it. It didn't get to the core of my transformation and my journey. It didn't have the grit and authenticity that reflected the real me. When I finished reading the manuscript, I suddenly got up and went to the sink to wash my hands. It was as if I had to scrub away the lingering debris of my old life. As I looked in the mirror, it dawned on me that I was literally letting someone else write my story – AGAIN!

I immediately went back to my computer and dragged the manuscript to the trash. I vowed then that I would never again let anyone write my story – literally or metaphorically.

Beauty Unbound is the raw story of how I hit delete on my old life and rewrote the new authentic version of the life I was meant to live. A beautiful life, unbound.

INTRODUCTION

Let's play a game. In this game, you have no choice but to play because it's already started. You aren't told the rules of the game until you break one by accident or see others break a rule. *The rules are different for different skin colors and genders – but no one ever tells you that.*

The only way to measure your progress in the game is to compare it to the other players. *Everyone starts with different advantages in the game, but everyone pretends they started with nothing.*

Oh, did I tell you that you never really can win? You'll always find another player who is doing better, and you'll spend your time, money, and soul trying to catch up.

Now, that doesn't sound like a game you would want to play if given a choice, right? But we all are playing this game right now. It's called life.

At forty-eight, after matching all the categories that would seemingly let me "win" this game, I finally realized I didn't want to play it in this way anymore.

Most of all, I realized I wasn't sure what I wanted out of life. Oh, I thought I knew the path to happiness; it seemed straightforward when I thought about it:

Do well in school.
Get a good job.
Find a good man.
Get married.

Have children.
Get a charming house.
Drive a fancy car.
Help your kids do the above.

From a young age, society and my parents instilled in me that this was my purpose. I believed this was *everyone's* purpose. I wanted what the Disney princesses like Belle and Ariel had. I dedicated my entire life to following that plan – and by the time I was forty-eight, I had achieved it. I had two wonderful children, a husband, a beautiful home, fancy cars, and two successful businesses: a medical practice and an aesthetic medspa. I expected to feel satisfied. Instead, I felt hollow. I realized I had never figured out what I wanted out of life, and that I was living a template of a "Best Life" that wasn't fulfilling for me.

It took me a lifetime to learn this, but deep down, we all know what we want and what we need; we know that it takes work and that it might not fit with what is acceptable to society. *That is when we feel the tug of our invisible chains. These are the chains that bind us to the game.*

These chains are the fear of the unknown, fear that we can't handle the change, and the biggest one – fear of judgment from our friends, family, and society. So, we settle for the next best thing, the life everyone accepts. A life that should make us happy but never really does. What life would you have now if you didn't worry about your ability to make that life or didn't worry about what other people might think? What could you accomplish when you trust that only YOU know what's best for YOU and that you can make it happen anytime you want – regardless of the perceived hurdles?

You are probably forming a picture in your mind right now, and you are probably laughing it off as a "fantasy."

I used to think that, too.

Today, I'm telling you that your disbelief is hardwired into you by external sources. I learned this lesson the hard way. I always thought something was wrong with me for wanting more. I was told it was in my best interest to follow the paths given to me by my parents, schools, romantic partners, and society.

What I wish I knew when I was younger is that you can live a life Unbound from all of these factors. Being Unbound doesn't look the same for all of us. We each have to figure out what makes us tick to figure out our own version of Unbound. Being Unbound isn't as easy as making a copy of someone else's life. That's just a way to live within the confines of someone else's expectations.

I like to call this copy approach "Personal Blanding." Personal Blanding is when we take something we see in someone else's life and try to apply that "brand" to ourselves with a slight modification. There is also a concept of blanding in businesses – when businesses seek to copy other successful businesses' marketing. What happens over time is all the marketing looks the same, no company stands out, and nothing is unique. That's what we, as humans, tend to do with our own lives. We try to copy someone else's, and then all of our lives look the same, and we end up unhappy because we're not really creating the life we wanted for ourselves.

It's never too late to live Unbound. I meet so many people in their thirties who are afraid to make changes. Which I find ridiculous because I am over fifty! By society's standards, my life is over. But you know what? Screw society! I am just getting started. My last name, Sundar, means beauty. I'm embracing that and removing all the invisible chains that have held me back to live a life Unbound.

Chapter 1

RELATIONSHIP BOUND

I valued my relationships, but what I realized was that my reliance on my relationships was one of the many invisible chains that prevented me from living an authentic life. I realized I did not know who I was without my relationships. My marriage had defined me in the past, but once that was over, I found I had a vacuum in my life. I instinctively just replaced it with countless other friendships and relationships. I traveled. I dated.

I'll admit, for a brief time, that made me feel free. But it wasn't real freedom. It wasn't freedom from my old life. It took me a few years to realize that I was still **bound**.

As human beings, we are hardwired to seek pleasure and avoid pain. Especially emotional pain. To avoid pain, many of us have succumbed to the pressures of society and have lost our ability to fight. I thought I was one of the fighters – when I was younger, I was always told that I was rebellious and difficult, and many times I was led to believe that I was doing things my own way – when it turns out I was just living a slight variation on the way society wanted me to live. Over the years, society had co-opted my rebellion and unknowingly taken the fight out of me. All my "hard won" freedom to live my life as I pleased still fell within the rigid confines of what was acceptable to those around me.

RELATIONSHIPS SHOULD NOT DEFINE YOU.

I have been peeling back layers of my persona for the past two years. I was a different person as a doctor, as a medspa owner, as a mother, and as a wife. I realized that, after forty-eight years, all these personas and roles were masks I thought were necessary for my life, but all they did was hide the real me. I wanted to be accepted and fit in. Early on, the layers came off easily and flaked off like an unsightly sunburn. It was embarrassing, but it wasn't going to kill me. Now, each layer comes off in strips and hurts more. The pain pierces deeper. Leads to more tears. It takes a lot for me to cry, but add wine and seclusion, and it happens more frequently. I have rebuilt my businesses, my self-worth, and my life. But I had to pull each of these apart and destroy them first. I painstakingly destroyed everything I had spent decades carefully crafting into a life I only *thought* I wanted. My marriage, my family, my career, and my very fragile self-worth had to be broken down so I could rebuild. That painful process started with how I was bound to relationships.

Like many women, I was defined by my relationship with a man for almost twenty-seven years. Even though the movie wasn't released yet, I went into marriage with the "You complete me" attitude from *Jerry Maguire*. It took me years to realize that although that seemed so romantic on the big screen, the idea is a complete fallacy.

My sense of self didn't exist without my husband, and not only did I look for him to complete me, I had also changed myself to become some version of me that was comfortable for him and for everyone else. That version of me took on a life of her own. I loathed *her*, yet I had to share my body with *her*.

RELATIONSHIPS ARE NOT ABOUT ENDURING; THEY SHOULD BE ABOUT GROWING AND FLOURISHING.

What defines a good relationship? For me, a good relationship was my duty to create, and I could only create a good relationship by enduring to honor what was expected of me. That's what my parents taught me, and that was what I was planning to do. Endure. By definition, *endure* means to remain in existence. Until death do us part. I was too young to know what I wanted in marriage, so I did what I was told was right. Endure. For almost three decades being a version of myself that wasn't really me.

Comparing a healthy, flourishing relationship to an "enduring" relationship is like comparing a flower to a weed. I didn't know who I was anymore because I never learned how to be grounded in my own values and principles within a relationship.

The Beginning of the End

What you are about to read is based on my viewpoint at the age of twenty-four. My husband and I were both young and had no idea how to communicate in a healthy way. I wasn't shown healthy marital communication by my parents; therefore, I didn't know the difference between a healthy relationship and an enduring relationship on my wedding day. I stood in front of my family and friends, reciting my vows and looking adoringly, and dutifully, at my future husband.

I remember standing there as the pastor recited the well-known verses from Corinthians 13. It is a common reading at a wedding because it describes how love, as a concept, should be. We tend to take this passage for granted because, of course, ***Love*** should be patient, kind, etc. When I looked at the passage again after my divorce, I wondered if I would have gone through with the marriage if I filled in my future husband's name in the blanks? Did we personally meet the requirements of "Love" as defined by Corinthians?

I rewrote the passage, removed the word love, and made it specific to what I should have expected from my spouse and from myself in my marriage. I never really paid attention to the words back then, but I wish I had. I might have done things differently. Here is the rewritten passage. Be sure to insert your name to make sure you are holding up your end of the bargain. Then feel free to insert your significant other's name, or maybe even a potential spouse, as a test.

______ is patient with me, ______ is kind to me. They do not envy me or my friends, and do not boast to prove they are better than me. They are not proud of themselves over me. They are not rude to me, are not self-seeking in the relationship, are not easily angered with me. They don't yell at me. They keep no record of my wrongs. They do not believe lies, but they accept hard truths. ______ always protects me, always trusts me, always hopes my dreams come true, always perseveres with me during difficult times.

It never occurred to me back then to expect more out of a relationship than comfort, security, and...a father for my children. I didn't understand or anticipate that needs and life direction could change in time. It turns out that, like most of us, I didn't really understand what real unconditional love was.

And so, with a great misunderstanding of what love and marriage should be, which is perpetuated by society, I went forward. I knew marriage would be work, but I looked forward to having the wedded "bliss" that we are promised. But my wedded "bliss" was fleeting, and I thought about divorce within the first month of my marriage.

> MOST OF US ARE UNPREPARED FOR MARRIAGE. IT REQUIRES AN UNDERSTANDING OF THE NEEDS OF EACH INDIVIDUAL, GOALS FOR THE RELATIONSHIP, AND EFFECTIVE COMMUNICATION.

Can you imagine? The ***FIRST MONTH***. Talk about buyer's remorse. And as far as I was raised, all sales were final when it came to weddings! There was no return or exchange period. I didn't have the skills to understand why I felt this way at the time, but I understand now that I have an instinct to quit a relationship the minute things get tough. It was my way of emotionally avoiding pain. I would go to that place often even when I didn't say the words.

I felt stuck. I couldn't get a divorce after a month of marriage. First, it is just plain RUDE. I was raised to be a polite young lady, like most of us. After all, what would all the wedding attendees think? Would I need to return all the gifts?

Secondly, how would my parents and in-laws deal with the embarrassment? How would I deal with the shame? It was too much to deal with. So, instead of thinking about divorce, I thought maybe I was making it out to be worse than it was. Women are always told that we tend to be overly dramatic and emotional, and I felt I was no exception.

There were things we agreed on, but we had different world views. When we disagreed, we fought nasty and called each other names. We said hateful things we couldn't take back. We kept a scorecard of each other's wrongdoings. I have a particular distaste for the word *bitch* since I have been called that by men when I have stood my ground (admittedly not in the nicest way). I heard it enough that I even labeled myself a bitch and felt ashamed to be one.

I yelled, screamed, and called him horrible names (because I was a bitch and that's what bitches do), and a toxic pattern emerged. Every time we tried to talk about things, our voices escalated, and often he would leave. Because he had a habit of driving fast and recklessly, I was concerned for his safety. I didn't want to be responsible for that, so I almost always conceded at that point. Emotional blackmail. It worked because every time he got upset, I stifled my voice and shut up to keep the peace. In hindsight, I don't blame him. Instead, I blame myself for not knowing better, and I blame society. Men have been shown by their fathers, other men, and by movies and popular culture that this is how "masculine men" express themselves. It is acceptable for men to express their anger using physical force on objects, raising their voices, and withholding affection. Women, on the other hand, are considered bitches when they express their anger. Society has one set of rules for men and another set for women. I was raised by a father who would withhold affection when I behaved in a way he didn't like, so I thought that was an acceptable quality in relationships.

I blamed myself for making life difficult for my parents by not being obedient, and now I was doing the same thing to my husband. People like nice girls who act a certain way, right? Those who go with the flow. Girls who are pleasant and sweet and don't demand equality, who don't stand up for their rights. My pretty face was a cover-up for the unlovable ugly person hiding on the inside. I always heard that I should be lucky to be loved, so I had to stay. I should be happy I found someone. Some people are alone forever, so who was I to dare to want more?

I thought about calling my parents and begging them to take me away from it all. Maybe they would understand and support me? But that wasn't the kind of relationship we had. They would have told me that marriage had its ups and downs, so I should accept the good with the bad, which is true to a point. I truly feel that all couples should have therapy before marriage to understand what each partner's needs are and how to communicate more effectively.

Chapter 2

NOT ALONE, BUT LONELY

I was married, but I felt alone. Because I was made to believe I had a shameful secret to hide. The secret was that I truly believed I was a bitch, and that no one would ever truly love me, let alone like me. That word, *bitch*, had clawed its way into my head and taken up residence in my brain. Like a weed, it sucked my self-confidence and would pop up whenever I was pushing for what I wanted out of life. It would just poke its head out and say, "Don't be a bitch."

I was taught that a woman should endure. I was raised not to quit or give up. So, I didn't. I endured. I sacrificed. And over the years, I lost myself, my self-worth, my courage, and my voice. I succumbed to the shackles of marriage ideals I didn't believe in just so it wouldn't make everyone else less uncomfortable.

Oh, and not to mention that the thought of being a divorced woman at twenty-four had its own stigma spiral that I wasn't ready for. Who would want to marry me once I was divorced? Despite the feeling in my gut that told me to run, I gave in to the voice in my head that created an endless supply of reasons why I should stay and play the dutiful wife. The real reality was that I was too immature for marriage. I didn't know enough about myself or life.

Each year, I became more codependent, losing more of myself and my identity. With each part of me that I lost, the fear of losing the man who made me feel whole increased. I got to the point where I would do anything to not lose him. I already changed my personality and my mindset and gave up more of my independence each year just to conform. And then the *coup de grace*: I wound up altering my body in hopes to please him and the rest of society. I saw that big breasts make a woman more appealing to a man. When I was in my early twenties, the bouncers let the big-breasted girls in while leaving us small-chested misfits to wait our turns. In medical school, I watched my male friends constantly ogle the girls with large breasts. Shows like *Baywatch* displayed Pamela Anderson's large, unrealistic breasts and blond hair as beauty personified. Magazines, movies, and MTV reinforced this. I surmised that to be beautiful and sexy I needed bigger breasts. I actually convinced myself that it was what I wanted.

WOMEN OFTEN GIVE UP THEIR VOICE. WE NEED TO UNLEARN THIS SO WE DON'T ABANDON OURSELVES.

Reflecting on this reminded me of the Disney movie *The Little Mermaid*. The main character, Ariel, wanted so badly to be human that she gave up her voice in exchange for legs. She fell in love with the prince when she rescued him from drowning. In his hazy memory, he remembered the beautiful voice of his rescuer. He knew instantly she was to be his wife. Ursula, the Sea Witch, tricked Ariel into giving up her voice by convincing her that men aren't impressed with conversation – they avoid it when they can. Ursula even tells her that "she who holds her tongue gets the man." We are subliminally told these things at a young age. It is constantly repeated in movies, in books, and in fairy tales. Young women are coveted for their beauty, but not so much for their intelligence and opinions. We are taught to please others and to give up parts of ourselves in doing so.

So, this young, impressionable Ariel, dying to get out of her father's kingdom to find freedom and true love, gives up her voice and her power. A bad play on her part because the prince actually was infatuated with the voice of his rescuer. The Sea Witch even tries to win the affection of the prince using Ariel's voice to lure him. How would the story have been different if Ariel had a voice and was able to express her needs and desires?

PERPETUAL SELF-SACRIFICE CAN BECOME PERPETUAL SELF-ABANDONMENT.

I continually sacrificed myself for the sake of the relationship because outside of the relationship I was lost. I didn't think I could exist on my own. I was told repeatedly over the years that I wasn't good with numbers or finances. Society and popular media reinforce these ideas. Therefore, as a woman, I wouldn't be able to manage the household finances. I was told in so many different ways that men are capable of doing many things women cannot do. I was brainwashed into thinking that, without him, I couldn't possibly manage the home, cars, and finances and have a full-time career.

Over the years, I realized our world views were so drastically different. I believe in abundance, but I was taught the scarcity mentality by my parents. I was determined to break out of this limiting mindset so I could live life to the fullest and in abundance. For him, money = stress. For me, money = security and gave me options and opportunities. Running a business stressed him out, and my ideas stressed him out. To keep the peace, I suppressed most entrepreneurial ideas I had because he said the ideas were far-fetched and required too much of a capital investment. Neither mindset is right or wrong; they are just incompatible.

How could I want more out of life when we had so much. Wanting more made me ungrateful by society's standards. A happy person would be grateful for what they had, right? I was grateful, but I wanted to live out my full potential. Women are constantly told we should not want more and that we should be "less than."

We should want less, talk "less," and be "less."

I don't think people are necessarily bad, but sometimes the combination of people can lack growth and create stagnancy. Thinking about divorce made me feel like a failure. I dreaded having to explain my decision to everyone. Especially because I didn't want to disappoint anyone. I was also afraid of being alone in the world. I was petrified that I was making the wrong decision, and I was tempted to stay in my comfort zone.

When you are tangled up in a relationship, it can sometimes affect all the other relationships in your life. I was taught that this relationship was the only important relationship in my life. Nothing else mattered, not even my relationship with my parents and siblings.

I had to work on rebuilding relationships with friends whom I believed would be supportive and started to rebuild the relationship with my family. I took more trips to see my parents, as our relationship had been strained over the years. I started visiting my brother more often, too, without my husband, and it was interesting how much better my brother and I got along and how much we had in common. I worked on building more solid relationships with my female friends. It took quite a bit of time and effort, but this support system was my lifeline. It prevented me from rushing into a romantic relationship out of loneliness.

Chapter 3

THE DISNEY DECEPTION

Every woman is raised to want the fairy tale. The Disney movie *Beauty and the Beast* was my favorite. I was a little like Belle: confident, slightly nerdy, yet rebellious. She stood out from the crowd and was a bit odd. She had the relationship with her dad that I wished I had. She could have married the perfectly handsome Gaston, but instead fell in love with a Beast. She managed to tame the angry beast and get to the prince hiding inside. I secretly hoped my life would play out like that, and I would have a "happily ever after" – except that's the part that Disney never shows us. They just let us assume that everything worked out perfectly. We assume that Belle and Beast never fight and are compatible forever. That's the Disney Deception.

FULFILLMENT SHOULD BE MORE THAN A PIPE DREAM.

Ten years ago, to the outside observer, my life looked like it was from the pages of a fairy tale. I was married to my first love and had two beautiful children, a beautiful home, expensive cars, and two thriving medical businesses. It looked perfect on the outside, and yet I just felt so empty. Every day held challenges, professional and personal, and I felt crushed by the weight of it all At work. At home. My practice was flourishing, my kids were well-adjusted and doing well in school.

But I wasn't flourishing or thriving. I was just existing and starting to wither. I longed for more purpose and direction. Everything suddenly seemed very small, contracted, and rigid. Not at all how I pictured my life would be at that point. I bet like me you thought happiness and joy were one and the same, but there is a big difference. Happiness has an external trigger. It is based on other people, things, places, thoughts, and events. Joy is cultivated internally and can only be present when you make peace with who you are and how you are. There is also a big difference between doing a job and living your highest purpose. A job provides you with the necessary finances to sustain you, but it doesn't fuel your passion. Joy comes with a sense of purpose. One could argue that I had a purpose – I was healing people and raising children. This was part of my purpose, but joy really comes from realizing your highest purpose. The reason you exist on this planet. I didn't find that until years later, but the search was an amazing journey. In order to find it, I had to uncover parts of me that were hidden away.

Women are programmed at a young age to want a life that we see in the movies. Real life is so different. In real life we have different fears, issues, and challenges. When I was married, my biggest fear was being cheated on by my husband and losing the love of my life. My biggest fear now is cheating on myself. I am fully prepared to disappoint anyone and everyone as long as I don't disappoint myself. Being with a man who doesn't appreciate me for who I am would be the biggest cheat of all. Rather than being afraid of losing a love, I fear losing myself. I am determined to not sacrifice myself for others.

Whenever I doubt my decision, I look in the mirror and recite my mantra: "I choose me." That is one of my favorite affirmations.

IT IS OKAY TO BE HAPPY WITH WHAT YOU HAVE AND WANT MORE!

In my medspa practice, I saw a lot of women who have similar struggles. They feel emptiness in their lives and try to fill that void with excessive food, drink, or exercise or by contributing to charitable causes. They do what they can to avoid that lonely, hollow feeling. The numbness you feel when joy slowly seeps out of your life. Knowing you could and should be something more. Until your brain chimes in and says, "Stop being ungrateful and be happy with what you have."

These women also have good partners who are committed to the relationship or family and are contributing members of society. I know my husband was. Initially, we were on the same path. We started a family and a business. I can't imagine a better father with whom to co-parent our sons. But as time passed, we didn't grow together like I had envisioned. Every year, we grew further apart. You see, I had different boxes for my relationship with my husband. There was the co-parent box, team player box, business partner box, and husband box. Many of the compartments worked well, others didn't.

When we first got together, we were in our twenties. A mutual friend in our dorm introduced us. I couldn't stand him at first. It was clearly not love at first sight. Opposites attract is what everyone tells us, and we were opposites.

If you take two very different people and add cheap alcohol, it's amazing what can happen. It's simple chemistry. The alcohol acts as a catalyst, which creates a chemical reaction by lowering the energy needed for the reaction to occur. Or, in this case, lowering my inhibitions. A catalyst can offer a new direction or chemical pathway in order to skip steps that require energy. Such as ignoring requirements that I had in my head for an ideal partnership. Catalysts can work in different ways. They can help large molecules combine and release a ton of energy, or sometimes they force a molecule to shift its own structure. Many years later, I'd find out that it did the latter.

And that was the start to our relationship. We immediately started to spend most of our time and most of our nights together. Based on society's rules, the next right step was clearly marriage and then children. But throughout our relationship, our core molecular structure shifted away from authenticity. This happens because this is what we are taught to do.

It is easy to overlook issues with your relationship when you are distracted with pursuing a career in medicine. Imagine just starting a relationship and suddenly having a dominatrix named Medicine join the relationship – she was demanding and thankless, taking more hours from me than I ever wanted to give. I didn't know it back then, but she was going to be a thorn in my life and relationship for a very long time.

Medical school was tough, but nothing compared to internship and residency. In a typical rough week, I would go into the hospital at 6 a.m. Monday, return home Tuesday night (usually late). I would eat dinner and pass out to recover from the night of no sleep before. I would arrive at the hospital early Wednesday morning and come home Thursday night. I would spend the weekend at the hospital from Friday morning to Monday evening. I had two nights at home to see my husband every other week. The following weekend I would be off, but I was so exhausted from the week before that I was barely functional. I was physically and emotionally depleted. People complain about a bad day of work, but they have no idea. A bad day at work for a doctor means someone died. It means that even if you do everything you can, there is blood on your hands, and you feel responsible. You replay every moment, every step, and second-guess every decision you make until you are physically sick. No one teaches you how to process this. I was in my mid-twenties and had never dealt with death. I couldn't discuss this with anyone because I feared I would be thought of as weak. When my husband wasn't home, I would curl up on the floor of our balcony in a fetal position after consuming enough alcohol to just cry. I have laid on the cold balcony floor in twenty-degree weather. The cold ground felt secure. My foundation was so shaky that this gave me some sense of stability. I never realized what I was getting myself into when I started down the path of becoming a doctor. No one prepares you for this part. And I was doing it all for thirty thousand dollars a year.

MEDICINE IS A DEMANDING MISTRESS.

The relationship with medicine was abusive from the beginning. It made me feel paranoid. I suffered from PTSD, and I didn't even know what that was. But medicine was seen as a path that many wanted to take. I remember thinking, *Who am I to question this path?*

I vowed I was not going to have arguments when I was home because we barely saw each other. It was difficult to learn better communication skills and put enough time and energy into our marriage when we saw each other so little. While I was working, he did his own thing, and I did mine. We met in the middle as much as possible before drifting further and further apart from each other and ourselves. I guess Medicine got what she wanted.

The stress and the demands on my time increased after I opened my medical practice, and it continued to worsen over the years as our viewpoints on business, life, and self-improvement continued to change. I never really gave it a second thought. I felt like this was "normal," and when I talked to friends, they all shared similar experiences and just said that spouses "doing their own thing" and having separate hobbies was how marriage worked. It probably does work for many couples. It just wasn't what I wanted from a relationship.

I finally got to the point where I felt alone. We were together but not *together*. We made efforts to have date nights so we could stare at each other silently while I longingly admired couples who seemed like they were in love. At that point, I thought I would have been more comfortable with a perfect stranger.

My relationship with my husband wasn't meeting my emotional needs, and I doubted that I was meeting his. Truth be told, all of us are emotionally needy when our needs aren't being met. This doesn't mean we are inherently broken or needy; it just means we haven't found the right fit for our needs. It also is not reasonable to expect another human being to meet all of your needs. Each person in a relationship should be responsible for meeting many of their own needs. This would have been very helpful to know prior to getting married. After reading several books, including *The Five Love Languages* by Gary Chapman, I finally understood some of the reasons why. My main love language is quality time. My husband's main love language was acts of service. It made complete sense that his idea of doing nice things for me was changing my oil and keeping up with the chores, but I felt emotionally disconnected because he wasn't spending quality time with me. He was too busy getting things done to make me feel connected. Both of our love tanks were empty, and we didn't understand why we felt this way.

Chapter 4

DIVORCE BOUND

From an early age, we are taught "quitters never win, and winners never quit." We are brainwashed with the idea that we should never quit because quitting is a failure. This is reinforced through popular media. Think about all the books, movies, and tv shows you have consumed over the years. When was the last time the protagonist walked away from a fight? Never. That's not what makes for a good "story."

We are expected to live heroically, and, as women, we should also live tragically. We are expected to endure. We are told from day one that we are weak. So, we endure so we can be seen as strong. We abandon ourselves regularly so we can be accepted, and, in that way, we can endure longer.

We are taught that quitting is the easy way out. The stigma of a quitter is something society has imprinted on our souls. We never want to be a dropout or a good-for-nothing loser who quits!

But what if enduring were actually the weaker, easier option?

WHAT IF QUITTING IS ACTUALLY THE BEST OPTION? WHAT IF IT IS THE PATH THAT REQUIRES THE MOST STRENGTH?

Sometimes we need to quit a marriage or the roles we have assigned ourselves. This is what I call the marriage mindset. I was going to embrace being a quitter for the first time in my life! The first thing I was going to quit was my marriage. I quit because to stay in the marriage mindset I created meant I had to set aside the personal goals I had for myself and had to constantly suppress who I was as an individual. My marriage mindset was keeping me stuck and was going to continue to keep me bound unless I made a change. Unfortunately, I couldn't figure out how to change that mindset while remaining in the relationship, so it was the only choice I had at that point.

I didn't make this decision lightly. My parents have been married for fifty years, and my in-laws have remained married for fifty-five years. A part of me wanted that, and a part of me wanted ME back. I wanted both, but I couldn't have both at that moment in time. As a science geek and a doctor, I spent countless weeks reading everything I could get my hands on about how to make a decision about getting a divorce.

After my research, I compiled a list of questions to ask myself to see if divorce was the right step for me:

1. Am I putting aside my personal goals?
2. Do I change my belief system just to please someone else?
3. Do I feel like I need my spouse because I am unable to do things on my own?
4. Do I have to change my appearance (through makeup or augmentation) to be attractive?

5. Do I have to be "quieter" to exist in this relationship?
6. Do I have to "nag" to get what I want?
7. Do I feel like I have to walk on eggshells?
8. Do I no longer have regular sex with my partner?
9. Am I isolated from my friends and family?
10. Do I live in fear of physical or verbal abuse, or fear that my spouse will hurt themselves?
11. Do I question my thoughts and decisions over and over again?
12. Do I feel like I have to be perfect and am not allowed to make mistakes?

I realized that somewhere along the way I lost my voice and surrendered my power to the relationship. As women, we tend to surrender ourselves and our voices for the sake of others. In doing so, we surrender our power to their whims. This is what society expects of us.

We have the choice between Fear and Self-Confidence. When I make the hard decisions in life, I now make them based on the trust I have in myself. When you trust your own decision, others will, too – because they will feel the confidence you have in that decision. I inadvertently blurted out the news that I was considering a divorce to my parents before I was even sure about my decision. I expected hesitation and expected them to beg me to reconsider, but what happened surprised me. They basically said it was my life, my decision, and that I needed to do what made me happy. I was pretty sure my parents were taken over by aliens at that point. These were NOT the same people who raised me.

It finally got to the point where I could no longer live the lie. Was I supposed to stay in this marriage where I had lost myself for the next few decades? Should I teach my sons that marriage is a death sentence or a choice for happiness? Should my life be martyrdom, or should I be a role model for my sons? I chose to be a role model for them as a mother and hopefully for the type of woman they would choose as a wife.

So, I decided to see how quitting worked for me. Because a life of never quitting was not helping me to be happy.

One day, when no one was home, I asked my oldest son, Roland, who was seventeen at the time, what he thought about me getting a divorce. His answer shocked me. "Mom, I can tell you are not happy. It's obvious. I definitely don't want you to stay married on my account. Derek will also be fine in good time. Do what you need to do to be happy." *Out of the mouths of babes*, I thought.

It still took me over a year after that conversation to actually say the words out loud. One morning, we had a fight about nothing, as was usually the case since we had grown so far apart. I let the dust settle and went outside to talk to him. I looked at him and said, "I still love you, but I want a divorce."

Just two months prior, I had moved out for a month to a condo on the beach to sort out my feelings. I moved out under the pretense of finding myself. Honestly, I thought I was turning into an introvert because I felt like I always wanted to be alone. I assumed I would just sit home at the condo and be miserable. On the contrary, I went out and socialized most of the time. I was actually happy! Laughing, smiling, and feeling free. The shadow of the old me was starting to emerge, and I liked myself. There were, of course, times where I felt sad, but mostly I was happy. My husband and I had two dates while I was away. I was excited to see him, but I was excited to see him leave as well. I returned home from being away for a month feeling relieved and excited. But a few weeks into my homecoming I felt despondent as my authentic self was getting buried before she had a chance to completely emerge.

PEOPLE DON'T REALIZE
THAT LOVE ISN'T ENOUGH
TO SUSTAIN A RELATIONSHIP.

I still loved my husband, yet I realized love just wasn't enough. You can love someone, and they can be completely wrong for you. I loved him but not more than I loved myself. I loved my children and didn't want to break up my family, but again, not in spite of me. I wasn't put on this earth to suffer for the sake of everyone else. I thought of all the reasons I should stay and all the reasons I should leave. I realized that this decision could not be made with a pro and con list. I remember asking my friend Lisa, and what she said really resonated with me. She said you just know from that deep down place in your gut that it's the right thing to do. No one else's opinion matters. A little voice in my head had told me this for a long time, but I just chose not to listen. I didn't listen because I wasn't ready to deal with what I knew I had to do. I wasn't ready to act on the decision and break up my family. I have been taught by society to believe it was the selfish thing to do. What society doesn't tell you is that sometimes self-love can seem selfish, and that's not a bad thing in a world where women are supposed to sacrifice themselves for others. You have to look out for yourself first before you can look out for others.

Unconditional Love

Love is emotional, and compatibility is logical. It is possible to be in love with someone who has different ambitions and life goals, but that doesn't make us **compatible** – as was the case with my husband. To this day, I love him for the life we shared and the children we raised together.

It may seem as if I'm blaming my husband, but let's be honest: we know that both men and women share in making a relationship work or not work. And I finally realized one of the major reasons my marriage didn't work. I never really knew what love was even though I thought I did.

I thought I loved my husband unconditionally. Or, more accurately, I thought because I loved him that the love must automatically be unconditional. I was wrong. My love for him was conditional. We're taught that we should love people unconditionally, but we are never taught how. Women are told to love our spouses and family unconditionally, but to hate ourselves for everything we do wrong in the eyes of society. Then, when we fail at loving someone unconditionally, we beat ourselves up even more. The first step in learning unconditional love is learning compassion toward ourselves and learning how to forgive ourselves. We need to love ourselves without excuses, without anger, without judgment. Then and only then can we do the same for others.

Because I didn't love myself unconditionally, my love for him would always be conditional. I loved him when he showed up in a way that made me feel good about myself. In reality, that wasn't his role. I needed to show up for me in a way that I felt good about myself. I hid behind the mask of success to avoid exposing my fragile self-worth. My self-worth was based on what I accomplished rather than who I was. I wanted to work toward feeling good about who I was as a person, and the truth was that I didn't like myself very much.

I used to think my inability to imagine living a happy life without my husband meant I was blissfully in love. I realize now that I resigned my identity and self-worth to the relationship in exchange for what I perceived, incorrectly, as a sense of purpose. This ended up becoming my insecurity because I sacrificed my individuality. It turns out we both did that for the sake of "love." I really wish someone would have told me that this isn't what love looks like. Damn those Hallmark and Disney movies. Damn their lies to hell.

In my situation, we both wanted such vastly different things out of life that, if we stayed together, neither one of us would be truly fulfilled. There would be no Hallmark or Disney "Love Can Conquer All" bullshit ending.

As I look at how differently we have chosen to live our lives apart, it is so clear that I made the right decision. I was vulnerable. Vulnerability is another concept that ended up not being what I was told it was. I was taught vulnerability meant weakness, but I wasn't weak! My weakness was forcibly purged from my body during my childhood and my residency. I later learned vulnerability isn't a weakness; it's a strength. It means being raw and accepting and not hiding your emotions or desires from others. Being vulnerable is beautiful and is the precursor to being free – to being Unbound. I desired to live the truest version of my life, and I wanted my husband to be able to do the same. Even if we weren't going to be together. And that, folks, is how I finally owned up to the true meaning of unconditional love and vulnerability.

Chapter 5

POST-DIVORCE UNRAVELING & REBUILDING

After the divorce, I learned so much more about the world and myself that I wouldn't have figured out within the sheltered confines of my "safe" and "comfortable" relationship. I was stuck in a box and itching to get out. I had so much to work on. So much self-discovery. Men had always told me I was overly emotional and emotionally needy, so I taught myself to hold back all my emotions and not feel. I numbed the pain of my emotionless life with money. I became a workaholic and was obsessed with making and spending money. Capitalism, like alcohol, made me feel better, but only temporarily.

At first, the thoughts of post-divorce and being alone, without my husband and kids, scared me to death. I remember calling my father sobbing hysterically: "I think I made a big mistake!" We tend to dwell on the perceived good of the relationship once a relationship is over. My father said to me, "Well, if you did make a mistake, you two will wind up back together. But whatever you do, give it one full year." This was great advice because, one year later, my ex-husband was in a new relationship. I would be lying if I said it wasn't a painful realization, but now I see they have a lot more in common than we did.

To dull the pain of loneliness, I traveled as much as possible. I indulged in travel to new places and had amazing experiences. I could feel myself growing in ways that I hadn't in decades. Travel worked well to dull the pain until I realized I was using travel to literally run away and to avoid being alone. I spent so much money and time running that I couldn't deal with bigger issues on my plate. I needed to be spending more time rebuilding my life for the future I envisioned.

Solitude was my biggest challenge, and it has taken years for me to embrace it. I have just recently learned to embrace quiet and solitude to think and to reflect on how I want my life to look. Instead of running, I now take more opportunities to look inward and address my deep-seated fears. Fear of the unknown, fear of being alone, fear of what others will think. Fear for our family, friends, and mostly our children. Fear will rule us and our lives if we let it. My old life was based on fear. Fear of losing our business, fear of not having enough money, fear that I would never find love again.

As women, we're conditioned to feel that when a divorce happens our life is over. I wasn't having that. As I went through my divorce, I documented what I like to call the "4 Stages Post-Divorce." Each stage is a different point in my own self-awareness and awakening. The first stages almost feel like the zombie apocalypse, where it can feel like we are part of the undead. That is because a part of us did die. And it has to die for us to rebuild ourselves and our lives. We must mourn not only the loss of the relationship but who we were in that relationship before we can move on to the next steps.

Stage One: Confidence & Appearance

WHEN YOU LOOK YOUR BEST, YOU DO YOUR BEST.

During post-divorce recovery, I struggled to regain my confidence and appearance. I suspect this may happen at the end of any relationship, but I haven't had enough to know. Divorce can be like a parasite, feeding off our self-confidence and self-worth. We are taught that women should be martyrs, giving up their lives to their husbands and children – and neglecting their appearance as well as their physical and emotional well-being. As women start to regain their confidence, they exercise more regularly, get cosmetic procedures, and enjoy life just for themselves. They seek to once again be attractive to the opposite sex.

Women, like me, often struggle to find their sense of self outside of the role of wife and mother. This is a loss of identity for most women. I was fortunate that I had a career, but I still struggled to find the real me buried under these roles. I had to start with a clean slate and evaluate my likes and dislikes. I had to establish different daily routines outside of what I had in my relationship. Because I lived in my marital home for a while, I replayed our marital routine for a long time until it started to feel foreign to me. It wasn't until I bought my own home and created spaces that were more reflective of who I was that I created new patterns of living.

I used to jump out of bed every morning racing through the day to accomplish everything on my to-do list. I was going through the motions without being fully present. How I start my morning now looks very different and more in line with my natural rhythm. I enjoy waking up to a peaceful routine and slowly ramping up as my day unfolds. I wake up early enough that I have time to snuggle with my dog and take a short walk in the beautiful city I live in. I sip my coffee so I can really taste it. I make time to stretch and feel gratitude for my life and the people in it. This doesn't happen by accident. This kind of life has to be purposefully created.

Stage Two: Loneliness

IT IS BETTER TO BE LONELY THAN TO KEEP THE COMPANY OF TOXIC PEOPLE.

Marriage and children kept me very busy. Every moment of my day was accounted for, and I had no time to think about anything more than getting through the day. If you add a career to that, a woman barely has time to breathe deeply, connect, or reflect. For me, it was important to spend the time post-divorce cultivating healthy friendships and outlets for loneliness instead of jumping into another relationship. I initially tackled the war on loneliness by writing out a list of twenty things I like to do. This way, when I got lonely, I had a list of things to choose from to keep my mind off being alone. During that time, even the thought of spending time alone filled me with anxiety. If I didn't have plans for the upcoming weekend, I felt a sense of dread and panic because I dreaded being alone with my thoughts and emotions. Distractions were welcome and very necessary for my sanity. I coped by being busy with people I barely liked, having meaningless conversations, and drinking a lot of alcohol. I did anything to avoid dealing with the uneasy emptiness of my new life. I felt like a fool for giving up everything I had for this new life of sadness and emptiness.

There was a point where I knew I hit rock bottom. It was the moment I sat by my pool, drinking alone. Everyone else had husbands and children to spend time with, but I did not. I found myself wishing that I didn't know how to swim. That way I could just drown myself. I guess I was just too lazy to come up with a better plan to end things. I wasn't really suicidal, but I knew I was in a pretty dark place if I was having thoughts like this. Deep down, I knew I had way too much to live for, and this was only a silly fleeting thought.

Stage Three: Finding My Own Identity

> TO REALLY FIND YOURSELF,
> YOU HAVE TO LOOK AROUND
> CORNERS AND CREVICES THAT
> YOU MEANT TO KEEP HIDDEN
> FROM YOURSELF
> AND EVERYONE ELSE.

Most of us change in a relationship. Sometimes we change so much we don't know where our significant other ends and we begin. We can get lost becoming so blended. I did this and lost track of my own identity. After my divorce, I would catch myself saying things I didn't actually believe anymore. They may have been true at one time, but my viewpoints changed as I evolved. As I became more comfortable with myself, I explored new ways of thinking. I became more open-minded in the way I viewed life, circumstances, and people. I was more open to becoming rather than being. I was more open to wondering rather than knowing. I surrendered myself to possibilities rather than being focused on outcomes.

I know women who carefully protected their own identities within a relationship. They maintained their own friends, hobbies, and sense of self. They had good boundaries where they shared things with their partner, but not everything. Unfortunately, I wasn't one of these women. I speculate that I wasn't this way because I was so young when I got married. Or, in part, because the relationships I witnessed were codependent. My culture insisted on codependency, so I didn't know there was another way. I didn't even consider the idea of maintaining my own sense of self because my parents had already squashed the person I was to get me to be the person they wanted me to be.

Just like when I was growing up, I learned early on that it was easier to keep the peace rather than fight back. It was easier to be liked when I didn't fight back. At that point in my life, all I wanted was to be liked and loved. Even if it was for all the wrong reasons.

Personal & Sexual Power

SEX IS PERSONAL. IT IS UP TO EACH PERSON TO DECIDE WHAT IT MEANS TO THEM AND HOW THEY CHOOSE TO EXPRESS THEMSELVES WITH IT.

When I was newly single, I approached sex as I did when I was a teenager. As expected, the dynamic played out accordingly. Because I didn't hold my own sexual power and sovereignty, I gave it away to each man. I wound up feeling rejected, hurt, and confused. I didn't even understand why for a long period of time. I went into each romantic situation trying to figure out how to keep a man – whether I wanted him or not. The goal was to hang on. Sheer stupidity. Apparently, this had become my life mantra, and I didn't even realize it. But remember, I had been conditioned to believe that keeping a man equaled success in life. Probably something I learned along the way from society.

I decided that that wasn't the key to a successful life. I needed to redefine romantic success in a way that worked for me. Why did I want a man? Did I really need a man? What do I stand to gain? What do I stand to lose? These answers will differ amongst women and possibly with each man they encounter. Nevertheless, these are questions that really need to be asked and answered.

I have noticed that my answers changed frequently and are now almost the polar opposite of what they were when I first got divorced. Early on, I needed validation, attention, and company. This made me feel secure and comforted. At one point, I was thriving on the drama of various situations I had gotten myself into (that is a story for another book). The drama made me feel excited and alive. Then there were the men who were "fixer uppers" or the ones with "great potential." These were huge time wasters. At one point, I even enjoyed the idea of changing emotionally unavailable men to the emotionally intelligent and evolved. Another futile attempt and a clear waste of time. I was clearly confusing chaos with chemistry over and over again. And all because I never had a healthy relationship role model. I made mistake after mistake and learned from each one.

Finally, after all of these experiences, I reclaimed my personal and sexual power. I felt at peace by myself. I stopped going out with men I had a bad vibe about. I stopped dating men whose company I enjoyed less than my own or that of my adorable puppy, Enzo. If I didn't feel like putting on makeup and showering to meet someone, there WAS a reason. I stopped dating for the sheer sport of it. I decided to date with a purpose. I finally understood what I was looking for. It wasn't always a relationship, but I always understood their purpose.

The dynamic continued to shift more favorably as I listened more carefully to my instincts. I was no longer going to settle. I had my vision of the kind of man I wanted to be with. If they weren't reasonably close to what I ultimately wanted, I wasn't wasting my time.

Chapter 6

DATING AFTER DIVORCE

WOMEN ARE SLUT-SHAMED SO THAT MEN CAN HOLD ALL THE POWER WHEN IT COMES TO SEX. ONCE A WOMAN ACCEPTS HER SEXUALITY, SHE CANNOT BE SHAMED, AND THE RESULT IS A REVERSAL OF POWER.

How many of you watched *Sex in the City* in the late '90s? My favorite character was Samantha, played by Kim Cattrall. She was a proud, confident, highly sexual woman who thwarted monogamy and did not like her relationships to take an emotional turn. Samantha never needed feelings to be a prerequisite to a sexual relationship – it could just be sex. Samantha was also a savvy businesswoman. Although she faced criticism, she never allowed it to sway her from staying true to herself. I loved her character in the show and started to wonder if my old-fashioned views on sex, which were forced upon me by my parents, might be limiting my happiness.

So, let's talk about sex…or, rather, a lack thereof after getting divorced. I never had to worry about lack of sex being in a relationship for so long – until now. I was raised by conservative Indian parents. And when I say conservative, I mean really, really old-fashioned and traditional. Conservative to the point where I wondered if I was a product of immaculate conception.

You see, Indian children are raised a certain way, need to behave a certain way, and should grow up to live a traditional life. High value is placed on education, professional success, marriage, and children. My parents never taught me about my body or sexuality. I learned everything through my friends, which is sometimes a really bad thing, because you only get the perspective through the eyes of another child. I learned all about menstruation, sex, oral sex, and homosexuality at school.

What I learned from my parents (and society) was that sex was a commodity a woman could give to a man. Kind of like money, but money you should be ashamed of having or using. You were supposed to be ***very*** careful whom you gave it to. According to them, each time you gave it to someone, YOU had less value. Basically, with each man you have sex with, your worth decreased until at some point you were worthless. In a nutshell, Chastity = High Worth. The opposite was true for a man. Men had all the power to "take" a woman's value. My parents made it clear that I wasn't supposed to have sex until I was married. Once married, you had sex only to procreate, appease, or please your husband. Sex was not something to enjoy. The rest of the plan involved staying married and monogamous for fifty-plus years until you died. The end.

Look, I desperately tried to follow my parents' plan, but as soon as I hit puberty, I had urges I couldn't understand. It would have been nice if someone explained this to me. I knew I wasn't supposed to, but I couldn't wait to have sex, and I certainly did not wait until I was married. I felt guilty, enjoyed the hell out of it, and wanted more. It took me years to stop feeling this way even after I was married.

EACH WOMAN HAS THE POWER TO DECIDE WHAT IS RIGHT FOR HER.

As an adult, I own the power to make decisions that are right for me. I finally got to the point where I could enjoy sex...because I was married. It took years to stop feeling like it was dirty. Then something in me shifted. I started to wonder if there could be way more enjoyment than what I was accustomed to. Maybe it could be okay to have sex that is a little dirty and a little kinky? But I felt guilty about having these thoughts and pushed them out of my mind.

Here is the thing about any part of you that you lock away far within the caves of your very being. It all has a way of resurfacing – with a vengeful intensity. I was bored with everything in my life. That doesn't mean I wasn't thankful and appreciative of what I had. I truly was, and I knew I was blessed. But being appreciative doesn't equal settling, and that's the mistake everyone makes. You can be thankful for all your blessings AND want more out of your life. That's the thing about YOUR life. You get to design it the way you want, and only you get to decide if you are happy with it or not. You get to decide if it's good enough for you.

I longed to wake up and feel exhilarated about my sex life, and for me it needed to be prioritized in a relationship. I wasn't sure about how I felt about marriage or monogamy for that matter. It was clear what everyone else thought about it but not what I really thought about it. I suspected I would find out through dating. Everyone else told me I needed time to process and be by myself first. But I thought I was ready. I figured I may make some mistakes or get hurt, but it was worth it not to live life numb. I made sure I was physically safe from assault and safe from STDs, but decided to tackle the process. For me, it was the right move. I get that it may not be for everyone.

I remember one day my husband and I were out. There happened to be a very attractive man across the room, and he was staring at me. I remember feeling surprised that this younger man was looking at me the way he was. I thought it was comical, so I mentioned it to my husband. He responded with, "Young men do not like older women." I reminded myself that I was, in fact, older and therefore not attractive to younger men and carried on.

Fast-forward to today. Most men I dated were quite a bit younger than me. The first man who came forward to profess his interest was *fourteen years younger* than me. For some reason, society has accepted women taking care of themselves but not men. Between treatments and skincare routines, women are aging much better than men. Maybe that was why I wasn't as attracted to men in my age range. Most of them looked older and worse for wear than their actual ages. Or it could be because I wasn't ready for a real relationship and suspected that "situationships" with a younger man were not going to last.

At fifty, society would categorize me as a "cougar." People like to use cougar as a derogatory term for a pathetic female over the age of thirty-five who desperately seeks some type of relationship with a man at least eight years younger than her. The derogatory term is due to the unrest society has about aging and sexuality. The assumption in our culture is that men value beauty and women value romantic stability. Other assumptions are that men have a higher sex drive and women do not. None of these assumptions are true in all cases. I have on numerous occasions broken things off with men younger than me because our sex drives were not well matched (i.e., they couldn't keep up with me!).

BEWARE OF THE LIONESS.

I do not want to be called a cougar. Not because it's a derogatory term (I've been called worse), but because I am a ***Lioness***. The alpha female.

I can hunt, protect, nurture, and serve (but not in a subservient way). I can be powerful and aggressive, yet soft and nurturing. Today's woman can be financially stable and enjoy life on her own terms with whom she pleases. She can keep the company of younger or older men depending on her needs and desires. The Lioness is the true ruler of the jungle.

Early on, younger men were a good fit because they were fun, energetic, and unencumbered by the constraints of older men. I specifically looked for younger men who were financially stable and didn't have children. Although everyone kept telling me I may want to raise children again – because society has a problem with older women who don't fall into the mother role – I knew I wouldn't want that.

Did others judge me? Hell yes, there was judgment. People judge you when your actions or decisions conflict with their own insecurities or make them question the way they live. It's not about you, it's about them. I decided that anyone who judged me self-selected themselves out of my life. It was an amazing process that wasn't as emotionally painful as I expected since I decided I wasn't attached to the outcome. The result was a group of amazing friends whom I accepted and who accepted me without judgment. We were all able to be authentic and unbound. The result was a significant increase in the joy I felt.

Everyone had an opinion about when I should date, who I should date, and how long I should stay single. There eventually came a point where, after dating for two years, I had worked on myself to understand what I was looking for in a partner. My objective shifted from self-discovery and finding out what I wanted in a partner to wanting a real relationship.

MEN AND WOMEN MAY SEEM LIKE THEY ARE FROM DIFFERENT PLANETS, BUT WE NEED TO COEXIST ON THIS ONE.

I decided to revisit some of the relationship books I had read in the past. One of the most well-known ones was *Men Are from Mars, Women Are from Venus*. As I re-read this book, I hit chapter three, and it gave me some ***serious*** pause. The chapter is about how men and women cope with stress. According to John Gray, "Martians (men) withdraw, while Venetians (women) become increasingly overwhelmed and emotionally involved."

In summary, to feel better, men go to their caves and solve problems alone. Women get together and openly talk about their problems. When a man is stuck in his cave, he is "powerless" to give his partner the quality attention she deserves. Apparently, it is hard for her to be accepting of him at these times because SHE doesn't understand how stressed HE is. I immediately flipped to the beginning of the book to see when it was first published. I expected it to be from the dark ages. But, no, this book wasn't written in medieval times. John Gray wrote this book in 1992. It was misogynistic then, and let me tell you, it did not age well. Men don't get some special exemption from putting in relationship work because they're "too stressed." Men and women both get stressed, and both often have careers. No one should have a hall pass to forego communication and hide in a cave. Men and women should work together in a way that each person's emotional needs are met. I can now understand why so many of the men I met had this viewpoint. This book was only one example, but I'm sure there are hundreds, if not thousands, of versions of drivel like this clouding the minds of men into thinking that, when they have friction in their relationship, the man can go into his man cave, and the woman will go chat it up with her friends, and everything will be perfect.

RELATIONSHIPS ARE THE BEST WAY FOR US TO LEARN ABOUT OURSELVES.

I decided I would only be in a committed relationship if it met all my needs and expectations and was a good fit for both people. As I mentioned, when I first started dating after my divorce, it consisted of a string of toxic relationships. Life has a way of kicking you in the ass and teaching you some life lessons along the way. Each "lesson" came in a pretty package, but each relationship had its own type of toxicity. It turns out toxic was the only type of relationship model I knew how to follow. It started with my parents, I recreated the pattern with my husband, and I kept recreating it until I figured out it wasn't healthy. In toxic relationships, two people are emotionally dependent on each other to get the respect and approval they can't give to themselves. In contrast, in a healthy relationship, the couple respect and approve of each other because they respect and approve of themselves. Basically, the pattern would keep repeating until I learned to approve and respect myself for the real me, not the person I was with my mask on.

My mask
    Ripped off
Wound aches
    I am exposed
But now I dare to be different
    I keep pushing all my limits
I'm a force of nature
    And now I am free again…

– *Force of Nature,* Kalpana Sundar

DATING CAN BE FILLED WITH DRAMA, BUT WE CAN LEARN TO HIT THE "EJECT" BUTTON SOONER!

I originally thought the toxic drama presented itself only in younger men, so I tried dating men closer to my age. I found consistently that there was baggage drama related to an ex-wife, a kid, or work. Sometimes all three. Typically, these three aspects of their lives were so encompassing that they couldn't manage anything else except to have a relationship that consisted of texting all the time. You see, texting incessantly is a cheap investment. It takes minimal time for them to text. They do not have to engage in a conversation or plan a date or time to spend with you. Beware of men who text incessantly without making any plans to see you. All of this was a form of drama. Why so much drama? Because toxic relationships need drama to survive. It creates the necessary conflict to generate a false sense of meaning for a short while.

After a bunch of these unsatisfying relationships, I decided to stop dating and work on myself. I realized I needed to get to the point where I could love myself unconditionally before I could expect anyone else to. And by ME, I mean all of me. The sweet parts, mean parts, sad parts, and emotional parts.

Early on, I used dating apps because my social circle was small immediately after my divorce. I met some nice guys on the apps, but most of them didn't have the grit or substance I was looking for. They were just a catalog of pretty faces and shirtless photos. They embellished themselves to look more appealing. I completely understand why they do it. After all, who would swipe right if a profile said "Emotionally unavailable. Looking for superficial interaction. Have serious mommy issues."? Instead, they say, "Looking for my best friend and lover," which is code for, "I'm horny, and I want you to believe I want a relationship." In the beginning, superficiality was exactly what I was after. Then I met a man with an interesting set of tattoos...but that's a story for another time. I've had many of my friends ask me to write a book about my experiences in post-divorce dating. Who knows? I may just do that.

Here, I'll just say that I am thankful for every man I dated because each one taught me something valuable. Not about them, but about me. I realized dating and sex wasn't about a checklist. It was about how I felt with that person, how we felt in each other's presence, and the connection. The union should bring out the best in both people while we are being authentic to ourselves.

I used to think that the end of a relationship was only significant and could only cause pain if it lasted a long time. I found out the exact opposite. Two of my shortest relationships ended up being my most painful ones. Loss is a part of life – and especially dating and relationships. What we learn in relationships defines our understanding of ourselves. When we lose a relationship, we lose that part of our identity within that relationship. With the end of each relationship, I evaluated my behavior and made the necessary adjustments.

Chapter 7

CANCER CROSSROAD & REVELATION

I wish I could tell you that changing your life was as easy as just washing your face. But, getting to the point where I discovered how I wanted to live my life wasn't easy. It wasn't a magical experience without pain or fear. It took a great deal of work and self-exploration. It requires feeling pain from the past – and understanding what has affected you and how. I had written down my memories of getting cancer years ago as a journaling exercise. I'd like to give you an inside view of my experience and the things I realized years later.

For me, the first elephant in the room that I had been avoiding was my cancer. When I finally revisited my journals, I saw the experience through different eyes. Surviving a major medical issue like cancer does a lot to your perspective. You see things differently. Some things become more urgent. Others, less so. For me, my perspective on life has been widening in the nineteen years since beating cancer. In a strange way, I am grateful.

I was thirty-four and literally six months into my otolaryngology practice. Otolaryngology is a fancy Latin word that means Ear, Nose and Throat. I spent fourteen years of my life devoted to becoming this type of surgeon. My days were regimented and planned to the minute. I woke up every day at 5:30 a.m. to steal a few minutes of quiet time to drink my coffee before the craziness of the day started. It was always rushed, but it was my ritual. It felt like heaven before the chaos began. My two boys had to be dropped off at daycare. I had rounds at the hospital and a full day of patients ahead of me. I knew I would race through my day as I always did, knowing that work was only the first part of my day. I didn't have time for anything extra. It was a whirlwind of stress, but I took it all in stride as if it didn't affect me. *Internalize.* It's what all doctors are trained to do, and what I later learned all women are forced to do.

The day flew by and, at 6 p.m., I started to dictate the first of thirty-five charts. I still had over an hour of work to do. Physicians are strange creatures by nature. We just perform routine self-examinations of random body parts while sitting idle or while multitasking.

Because I am an ENT, I put my hand to my neck – and I felt something. A nodule. On my thyroid.

I thought, *What the hell is that?* That single nodule was a bit bigger than a centimeter. I continued to feel the rest of my neck. Nothing. A single nodule. And that, you see, is more likely to mean cancer.

I immediately found myself not wanting anyone to know that I had a health concern, but I decided to reach out to my colleague and friend to examine me. "I wouldn't worry about it," he said. "It's most likely a benign nodule." Even though I liked what he was saying, I knew better. My gut chimed in and told me I'd better get a biopsy.

I always did everything I could to avoid being vulnerable. I was trained in a male-dominated residency where vulnerability equals weakness, so I only saw it as a weakness.

Doing my own biopsy would be more efficient than taking the time to go to a doctor. Most of all, no one would have to know there was anything wrong with me or worry about me. I would just stick a needle in my neck in front of the mirror, get some cells, and send them off to pathology.

So, I told myself lies to keep from feeling vulnerable. I now see it as the lies we tell ourselves every day to get through things.

I had my medical assistant stand by me just in case something went wrong, and I did it. Well, I tried to do it. I wound up not getting enough cells, so I was forced to make an appointment for an ultrasound-guided biopsy at the hospital.

The interventional radiologist (let's call him Corey) was a friend and neighbor of mine. I arrived for my appointment and waited for my procedure.

Corey cleaned my entire neck with an antiseptic solution to prep the area. He felt around and found the nodule on the left side with the ultrasound. Then came the needle and some pain. The procedure was complete, and I would just need to wait for test results.

It would seem like that was the easy part, but fear consumed every moment I was awake, even while I was seeing patients and spending time with my kids. Thoughts of dying and leaving my young children for my husband to raise alone or with another woman.

When the results finally came back, sure enough, I had papillary thyroid carcinoma. The cancer diagnosis I did not want. It helped to have something to focus on like an action plan, but it certainly didn't change the fact that I was afraid.

At that point, I had to get my head together. The cancer needed to be removed, and I needed surgery. So, I contacted John, a head and neck surgeon in Gainesville, Florida. I knew him because I referred my big head and neck cases – the long, major surgeries I wasn't doing anymore – to him. He was a fantastic surgeon and the only one I trusted.

"How are you, Kalpana?" he said as he got on the phone. I remember feeling relieved. "So, what do you have for me?" he asked, assuming I had a patient to refer to him. I hesitated, took a deep breath, and said, "It turns out I've got papillary thyroid carcinoma." There was a bit of a pause. "Well, we will get you into the office ASAP and get this taken care of," he said. I arranged for my consultation and surgery, and made sure I had call coverage and coverage for my patients when I was recovering. I kept reminding myself that it was a fairly routine procedure – one I had performed many times before.

Except there was an unexpected problem. The tumor was stuck on the recurrent laryngeal nerve, the vocal cord nerve, to the point where John had to actually strip the tumor off the fragile nerve with his scalpel, which could have resulted in permanent issues with my voice. I remember waking up from anesthesia with John standing beside me. "Count to ten, Kalpana." He was relieved to hear my voice sounding normal.

Then there was another problem. My calcium level dropped. It's just one of those rare things that can happen after thyroid surgery because the parathyroid glands are right behind your thyroid gland, and they control the calcium levels in your body. Although the glands weren't removed, they are delicate and can be ornery. If you touch them during surgery, they can get stunned and stop producing calcium.

ARGUING WITH YOUR DOCTOR MAY NOT BE THE BEST IDEA, EVEN WHEN YOU ARE A DOCTOR.

The next morning, my calcium was barely normal, and I knew John was going to keep me another night. I wanted to be in my own home with my kids, so I argued that I would get my bloodwork done first thing in the morning. If any issues arose, I would clearly know how to identify, address, and deal with them. After all, it's not like I'm not an ENT doctor… So, like an unruly, noncompliant patient, I left the hospital against his better judgment and mine. All because I wanted to go home and see my kids.

I should have known better, but all I knew was that I wanted to go home. My parents had my kids, and I ached to see them. I missed them terribly. I wanted to see their faces, hug them close, and take in their scent. There's something primal about the bond between a mother and her children, and I was feeling the tug of those bonds acutely. I also hated that we had to impose on my parents to watch our children. Not that they minded at all, they didn't, but it's just that at that time in my life, it was so difficult for me to ask anyone for help, even family.

During the night, my calcium dropped again. I woke up with tingling in my fingers, and I jumped out of bed and ran to the mirror. I was looking for something called Chvostek's sign. You know you have Chvostek's when you tap on your facial nerve and get this really weird facial tick. If you have it, it means the calcium level in your blood is dangerously low. I tapped. I had it. It was time to get to the hospital quickly.

Even though panic bubbled inside me, I forced myself to breathe and keep calm for my family. No one else needed to see me panic. I always internalized my feelings for the sake of others, and today was no different. It's something I know we all do as women. But it also came with the realization that I had to be strong for the family. I couldn't show vulnerability – I had to just keep going.

On the way to the hospital, my symptoms were worsening quickly. My fingers were starting to contract, my breathing felt more effortful. Shortly thereafter, my words slurred as I started to go into tetany. I knew I needed intravenous calcium gluconate – fast. I called the hospital to let them know I was on my way, hoping it would be ready.

I walked into the emergency department looking like the Hunchback of Notre Dame. Lance, one of my favorite nurses, saw me and quickly grabbed me. He was one of those nurses who could get an IV in quickly. My muscles immediately relaxed as the calcium went in, and all I could think was, *Oh my God. I'm going to live.*

At first, I did what many cancer survivors do, which is not dwell on what just happened and reacclimate to life. I dealt with the physical aspects of my experience since they were easier to deal with, and I ignored the emotional ones. There was a visible scar from the surgery on my neck, but no one could see the scar on the inside, including me. I buried the whole experience, because that's just what doctors are trained to do and what women have been forced to do to survive our days in an overbearing, male-dominated world. As a doctor, nearly every patient's problem is serious. If we dwell on one, we'd have nothing left emotionally to deal with the next.

THE EMOTIONAL REPERCUSSIONS FROM CANCER CAN TAKE LONGER TO RESOLVE THAN THE PHYSICAL ONES.

I went straight back to living the life of a dutiful wife and mother, and I went straight back to work. I was both consumed and caged by everyone's expectations that I would go back to doing it all. I took virtually no time off despite not feeling my best physically or emotionally. After all, I had a practice to run and patients to see, and I was the only doctor. I *was* the business and had no back-up. If I didn't go in, my employees wouldn't have jobs, my patients wouldn't have a doctor, and my family's income would be significantly decreased. That's a bigger burden than I realized it would be.

I thought I was doing the right thing until my body started to tell me I had missed an important part of my emotional recovery. The external scar had healed beautifully, but there were open wounds underneath. My body just told me to *wake up* and figure it out. Literally.

I had attacks of panic and claustrophobia that I'd never experienced before. I would awake from a dead sleep with the sensation of being strangled and gasping for air. I'd step into an elevator, and I would feel the walls start to close in on me as the doors closed. There was a prevailing theme to all of this: I felt constricted and trapped. What was making me feel this way? Where in my life was I constricted and trapped?

That started the next phase of my journey. I needed to go back and relive my cancer experience to process it. I started to learn a great deal about how I was bound – by society, by relationships, by fears, and by expectations. The responsibilities and demands of being a woman who is also the primary breadwinner are more overwhelming than most people give us credit for. If I, as a woman, fail, it will be used as a reason why women shouldn't be business owners or doctors – we are held to a much higher standard than men in the same roles. Men are given the opportunity to fail and bounce back. Society allows them to be weak and vulnerable, because behind every great man is a woman to support him. They have us as a support network. Behind every great woman, unfortunately, is a group of people waiting for her to fall.

As women, we are treated by society like those parathyroid glands, those tiny, fragile, glands that stop working if they receive a little shock. Instead of supporting us, we are avoided. When we fail, we are dead to the world and useless.

I realize now that I felt this way because I didn't have the right support network. In times of stress, I volunteered to remain strong for everyone else. I didn't focus on my mental wellness or my needs after such a devastating experience. I brushed them off. I have since learned that I need to have a good support network, and I need to be able to be vulnerable without being treated like I was fragile. Most of all, because I survived, I should ask for more out of life. Much to the contrary of what society would have me believe.

I now realize that for years, for all my life, really, I've surrendered my power and allowed others to direct me and control my happiness. Each decision I made, based on what others wanted, served to enclose me like an egg in a shell. I started by conforming to my parents' hopes and desires for me, then to society's constraints on my gender and my sense of self, then to the demands of my job, then to society's expectations of what family should be like, and finally to preconceived notions of what I should be happy with.

I needed to look at my life to find what my needs and wants were, as opposed to what others thought they should be. I needed to identify what my goals were for myself, my marriage and family, and my career. In short, I needed to uncover and unravel myself. All of me. The good, the bad, and the ugly, because they were all parts of me. I needed to become unbound. Revisiting my cancer experience brought that into focus and, in a strange way, gave me the tools to focus on myself and slowly remove all the things that bound me.

From this time of introspection, I created a framework for freeing myself called Beauty Unbound. And I started to dive deeper into all my experiences to see how I was binding myself to everyone's expectations of how I should act or think.

Chapter 8

BEING A DOCTOR SUCKS

We spend one-third or more of our life at work. For most of us, work is the foundation that defines us. If we aren't happy in our career, other areas of our life will suffer. We have more career options than ever before, the ability to learn and take courses online in almost any subject, yet more than seventy percent of people say they aren't satisfied with their careers. In fact, many of you reading this book right now may feel the same way about your profession.

How did we all get here? When I first started on my journey to become Unbound, I found myself at a crossroads. I am an accomplished surgeon; I spent my entire life training and working to be a surgeon. Why did I hate it so much? Isn't this what I wanted?

SO MANY OF US CHOOSE OUR PROFESSION FOR THE WRONG REASONS. THE CHOICE SHOULD BE MADE BASED ON PERSONAL FULFILLMENT.

To get an answer to that I had to dig far back into my memories. There are certain professions that Indian parents guide/push their children into. Medicine. Law. Engineering. As children, we most often strive to make our parents happy. I don't recall ever really wanting to be a doctor on my own, but I do know that I wanted to connect with my father and very much wanted to make him happy. And that wasn't easy. I already started out wrong because I didn't arrive on this planet with a penis, and I was dark-skinned. For an Indian family, having a first-born son is extremely prestigious. A son with light skin would have been an added bonus, and I was none of these things.

My father is a very responsible man. Very moral and a bit stoic. Even though he was, and is, very stable, he was not able to be around the family as steadily as other fathers. We started out as a family in Bangalore, India, and through my father's efforts, we emigrated. He had the vision and foresight to know that he could make a better life for us if we were in America. He grew up in poverty after his father died, and he wanted better for his family. So, shortly after I was born, my father left for the United States. My mother and I didn't join him until ten months later. It was a tough time for them because it was so difficult to communicate. Back then, it could take three weeks for a letter to get back and forth from the U.S. The fact that he left to try to create a better life for us was, of course, not appreciated by me as an infant. I can only imagine that the feeling of disconnect and abandonment I carried in my subconscious mind throughout my life began right there. That belief resonates with me. I believe those early feelings informed choices I made throughout my life. It created a theme, one that saw me through most of my childhood and directed me even in my adulthood.

My father was a brilliant engineer and he was often called upon to consult on different projects. Which meant he went wherever he could make the most money. Whenever we reunited, my father left. For the same reason, of course. He left to create a better life first for my mom and me, and later for my younger sister and brother. I suspect my father's leaving affected me and my life because, even on a subconscious level, all I knew was that he left – even though his intentions were good and his reasons valid.

In retrospect, trying to connect with my father was actually the reason for becoming a doctor. I remember intentionally trying to make a connection with my father when I was about five years old and he was sick. Nothing major, but he was the sickest I ever remember him being. Seeing him that way was a little scary for me. I remember wanting to help him get back to the way he was before.

That's when it happened: I told my dad I wanted to be a doctor so I could fix him. Somehow that statement was met with a lot of positive feedback. I could feel his happiness when I said I wanted to be a doctor. As soon as that happened, I bit on the career hook, line, and sinker. That was what I was going to do – because I needed to. I felt like I needed to win his approval. That was how I was going to connect with him, and he was the one I always wanted to connect with.

As I grew into my decision, I liked the idea that medicine was a very good field, one that was very respected. Just the thought of being a doctor would get me excited, too. I just don't know if it was always for the right reasons. The thought would get me excited for the prestige and the recognition. I also liked that the idea of being a doctor felt very benevolent. I'd be doing good things for people. I did like those aspects of medicine. The ability to help people was very important to me, but I always wanted to make a bigger impact on the world. How could I possibly do that being a doctor? It seemed fairly unlikely, but I pressed on with my career goals, and everyone was happy.

PARENTAL EXPECTATIONS ARE USUALLY WELL-INTENTIONED BUT CAN CREATE A NEGATIVE EMOTIONAL IMPACT ON CHILDREN.

I made sure I got good grades and stuck to the protocol, but there came a turning point where things became difficult. My parents started seeing my progress and wanted to tweak it to make it perfect. Things got to the point where my parents expected a certain level of grades. All A's and no B's. They wanted me to study all the time and limit phone and personal interactions with friends. I truly wanted to comply, but I, unfortunately, am rebellious by nature. I wanted to be me a little bit, cut loose every so often, and have fun – but that just wasn't allowed in my family.

We say a parent's love for a child is unconditional. That is usually a lie we tell ourselves to feel better. My parents' love for me was always conditional. Love and acceptance were withheld if you didn't behave or do what they wanted. I was not loved unconditionally and didn't know how to love unconditionally, which ultimately affected my marriage. The more I felt like I had to be a "good daughter" robot, the more I rebelled. It was stressful to be this model-perfect child so my parents could tell their friends what a great kid I was and that I was going to be a doctor.

Then, one day, I inadvertently upped the ante. I think I was in the fourth grade. I had written a report of some kind at school. It was about the heart. I got an A+. I showed it to my dad, and he was so excited. This reaction was the best one I had seen, so I said, "Maybe I should just be a cardiothoracic surgeon?" And, oh, how my dad's eyes lit up. I remember he said, "How impressive it would be to have a female surgeon in the family!" And I thought, "Oh, okay. That was better feedback than I expected." It was that approval – that pride and approval – that I was seeking to replace the feeling of abandonment I carried with me my entire life.

I became like Pavlov's dog. Anytime things weren't going well or I didn't feel connected to my dad, I would start talking to him about getting into medicine. Immediately, everything would improve. I was good to go.

A career in medicine does not give you the freedom to change careers. Mostly because it takes so many years and so much money to get trained. And the training is very specific. The typical doctor gets out of medical school and residency with a debt burden of $200,000, as of 2018. This debt keeps you bound and makes it difficult to change careers. The more expensive your education, the bigger and tighter the handcuffs.

THE HARDEST HANDCUFFS TO REMOVE CAN BE THE "GOLDEN HANDCUFFS."

For years, I knew I didn't want to practice medicine anymore, but I didn't think I had the freedom to leave it. My family depended on my income, so I had to do what I needed to do until my kids were older. Luckily, once they were older and college was paid for, I realized I could start making some changes.

Every year, the ENT practice had more constraints as mandated by the government and insurance companies. Professional satisfaction is at an all-time low. In the past, physicians were paid cash for service. The patient came in for a visit and paid the bill. Those were the good old days, where doctors' expertise was still valued.

Rise of Greed & Insurance Companies

In the last fifty years, the binding of doctors began. Third-party payers (the insurance companies) came along to minimize payments to physicians to the point that they could barely cover their expenses. Physicians had to work longer hours, see more patients, and devote less time to each one. Physicians are required to obtain permission from the insurance companies to order tests and perform surgeries. There are guidelines that need to be followed before the insurance company will authorize anything. This results in physicians feeling second-guessed, increased frustrations, and delays in patient care. As a surgeon, a peer-to-peer review is often necessary for any surgical procedure being performed. Records are requested, and then the surgeon needs to discuss the case with another doctor from the insurance company to get authorization for the surgery. The physician is often not a physician from the same specialty with a similar experience profile. I have spoken to family medicine physicians, emergency physicians, podiatrists, and OB/GYNs to obtain permission for ENT surgeries. They have no training or experience in treating patients in my field, but they have a checklist to determine whether the surgery is authorized. If only it were that easy.

Then comes the increased frustration of EHR, electronic health records. Entering and retrieving information is arduous, and the amount of information necessary in each patient encounter becomes ridiculous, making physicians feel like data entry clerks required to check boxes to get paid. Regardless of how well physicians document, it still takes forever to get paid by the insurance company. Often, it can take up to three or more months to receive full payment – if you even receive it. Insurance companies make physicians jump through more and more hoops to get paid below fair market value. This reduces cash flow for practices while increasing expenses. This is a perfect scenario for hospitals to buy independent practices and employ physicians, further reducing control each physician has over their personal and professional lives. More than ever, physicians are dissatisfied with their lives and careers.

Changing Careers

Changing careers is a difficult process, and transition is never easy. Even when I was in medical school, I spoke as if medicine would be my first career. I always said I would retire at fifty. Looking back, I realize these statements came from a place of knowing rather than a place of wishful thinking. A few years ago, I researched a bunch of career options for physicians who don't want to practice clinical medicine, but I couldn't find a career option that would make me feel fulfilled. All the options involved being an employee, like teaching or working for an insurance company. After so many years of being self-employed, I knew that wasn't a good fit for me. I needed the freedom to set my own hours, work in bursts, and travel on a whim. I didn't want to trade one pair of shackles for another. I still had an unrelenting urge to do something amazing with my life and make a big change in the world. It had to be bold and audacious. Being a surgeon just wasn't it. I wanted to make a career change, but I felt like I couldn't because I was bound to being an ENT doctor – I had invested most of my life on that path. So, I did the next best thing at the time, which was open a medspa as part of my practice so I could pursue my love of skincare and skin health as a "side business."

I called my medspa Avanti to pay homage to my Indian heritage, and because Avanti means "to move forward," which I felt would help me feel like I was able to pursue my passion, even though I was still shackled as an ENT doctor.

As time went on, I discovered that medspa and skin health were things people really wanted to see more of. I started to see the possibility of growing the medspa, but whenever I discussed it with my husband, he pointed out that we made a majority of our income from the medical practice, and it would be foolish to give that up. But I had my doubts about the medical practice due to the way that insurance companies had all the control of the money coming in.

In direct contrast to this system, the medspa industry is fee-for-service. I would often see patients who complained about a $25 dollar copay in the ENT practice spend thousands of dollars on cosmetic services. I don't believe this phenomenon is the fault of the patients.

After all, the insurance companies have done a great job of devaluing the services that a physician provides.

I decided I should stay as an ENT doctor because everyone was telling me that it was a sure thing, and it would be crazy to trade the known for the unknown. I once again abandoned myself, my needs, and my truest desires. With that small side of the business starting to grow, I saw an opportunity to push my passion a little more. I made a business case for starting a clean skincare line. The skincare line that we had in our spa was expensive, and while it was effective, it was full of parabens and ingredients that were known to be toxic/cancer-causing.

I wanted clients to have a non-toxic, effective alternative to the chemical-laden products that were available. I decided to call it Kalvera. A combination of my name, Kalpana, which means imagination, and Veritas, Latin for truth. The products did well in my medspa, and I envisioned healthy skincare options for every woman.

One day I was working in my medspa and had a revelation. The "aha" moment came when I was talking to one of my clients. She was complaining about another medspa she had been to while she was out of town. "They used 60 units of Dysport when you only used 30!" I explained that every medspa has a different approach, and that I had refined my approach over the years and took a more data-driven approach to treatments. I focused more on results and the healthiest long-term approach instead of selling more units. My client said, "I wish more people took your approach. It's unique, has integrity, and it works!" Her saying that rekindled an idea I had been pondering for years. I decided to run it by one of the people I respected most when it comes to business strategy – my younger brother.

WHEN VETTING A NEW BUSINESS IDEA, IT IS ALWAYS HELPFUL TO GET OTHER OPINIONS, BUT ALWAYS MAKE SURE YOUR OPINION IS THE ONE THAT HAS THE HEAVIEST VOTE.

You might think it's strange that my younger brother is who I turn to when I have a business idea. He's eleven years younger than I am, and he was always a sweet, kind-hearted, and fun-loving boy. As he grew up, he remained sweet and fun-loving, but had grown into an accomplished C-level executive with twenty-plus years of experience in multiple industries in startups and Fortune 500 companies across the globe, including Silicon Valley. He's the guy people turned to when they needed a completely fresh perspective on business. He spends his free time mentoring women and people of color in their careers and on starting businesses. He is someone who has been successful in building companies the right way: treating people with respect and focusing on profit and community at the same time. He's even spoken on those topics at conferences around the world – London, Paris, and Milan. I felt my idea had legs, but he had the business and strategy experience to know if it was possible to be profitable. So, I called him on a Saturday morning and told him what I was thinking.

He listened and didn't say much. He just said it ***sounded*** like a good idea but wanted to research it a bit. He'd let me know what he thought sometime later when he had time. I know he's a busy guy, so I assumed he'd get back to me later that week. Imagine my surprise when I heard back from him later that night! I was heading out on a date when I got a text from him asking to schedule a call in the morning. "That's odd," I thought. "Why is my brother texting me to schedule a call?"

It all made perfect sense the next day. He was treating it as a truly legitimate business discussion. Not just a chat with his older sister.

The idea I proposed was a franchisable, turnkey solution for physician-owned medspas that focused on data-driven skin health solutions. He spent the next few minutes explaining the research he had done on the industry. The biggest thing that would make this a successful business was to build the company with the unique values, processes, and data-driven approach I had cultivated over the years in my medspa practice.

He then went on to say, "It is a really strong idea – from my research, the medspa and skincare industries have been proven to be profitable, but there are still customer problems to be solved. Skincare is confusing for most people, and the definition of a medspa is nebulous – most medspas do everything from skincare to hormone therapy and even weight loss solutions – and their profit margins aren't as good as your current medspa. There is a large gap in the market for skin health-focused spas that use data to demystify the skincare process and achieve results for the client. To build the kind of business you are looking to do, you would need a co-founder with marketing, operations, HR, and tech experience to execute this. And I think that person should be me."

I sat silent on the other end of the phone not sure if I was hearing things correctly. A part of me was exhilarated that my brother believed in my idea so much that he was willing to quit his current job and build this with me. I liked the idea of building a company with someone I loved and admired, who had a complementary skillset, and who was also passionate about health and healthy skin.

The other part of me was panicking. My mind was racing with worries about how we were going to make this work financially. It would totally be my fault if my idea bankrupted my brother when he could have spent the next few years gainfully employed with a high executive salary at any company he chose. I was also worried about what my parents would say. Surely, they would say this was a ludicrous idea. Last but not least, what if this destroyed our relationship?

Somewhere deep inside me, I was able to focus on the part of this that felt right. I got past the fears, worries, and opinions of other people. I was able to break that invisible chain that bound me.

I always suspected that my brother and I would do something amazing together, and this is what it was. I had always wanted to build something big, something that was bigger than just a business. I wanted to build a movement. I wanted to build a company that helped women feel confident in their own skin. Society and my peers had led me to believe that I was crazy for wanting anything more than what I had already achieved. Now, my brother and I were actually going to build it.

We were about to embark on a journey of a lifetime. Together. And on that day, Kalvera Skin Therapy was born.

Chapter 9

COMPARATIVE BEAUTY

What is beauty? The concept of beauty has changed throughout the decades and differs from various cultures and perceptions of the world. The concept of beauty has been described, depicted, and drilled into our minds since the day we were born through pictures, radio, advertising, and interactions. Beauty has been defined in so many ways. Beauty is distorted and confused by conflicting messages. We are told to not be fat, or too thin, or too tall, or too short, and to have big breasts and athletic bodies. What I have learned is that the concept of beauty is simple. Beauty is confidence. Confidence is beauty. To be beautiful, we need to find confidence in ourselves and lead with that.

WOMEN OFTEN STRUGGLE TO FEEL GOOD ABOUT THEMSELVES BECAUSE WE WANT TO BE PERFECT. ONCE WE LEARN THAT OUR BEAUTY LIES IN OUR IMPERFECTIONS, WE LOOK AT OURSELVES DIFFERENTLY.

Even though I pretended for most of my life to really like myself, I honestly didn't. I wasn't comfortable being myself. I spent most of my life on the surface pretending and being what others wanted me to be. I never embraced my uniqueness. I already didn't fit in being a minority female, so I didn't want to make anything worse. I molded my personality into something more acceptable. The real me was buried in those layers I have stripped away, little by little, to finally reveal the core of me to the world. I won't lie. I felt vulnerable, afraid, naked, and a little raw when I started this journey.

There were parts of me I was comfortable with and parts that I wasn't. I am 5'1" tall, but, for some reason, my height never bothered me. Others would point out that I was short (as if I didn't know), but it never unnerved me. If I could have changed the color of my skin, I would have. The irony was that everyone I met wanted my skin color, but they didn't know the baggage that came with the "all-year tan."

My hair is "ethnic," so it is very wavy. All my life I tried to tame it to make it calm and straight like Caucasian hair. I would blow-dry it, curl it, and do all kinds of things to it. For some reason, this year, I realized that this is part of who I am, and I embraced it with a minimal hair routine. I let my hair just be in its wavy glory. Parts of my hair are tame, and the rest is wild, curly, and a bit unruly…just like me.

When I was younger, I remember being happy with my breasts even when men would constantly ogle women with large breasts. It seemed so shallow – as if a woman had nothing to offer but breasts. Later in life, I let the status of my breasts affect my self-worth. At the age of forty, having nursed both my children, my breasts started to sag, as would be expected. I felt self-conscious and embarrassed about my body because it was continually becoming less perfect. To soften the blows of insecurity, I decided to get breast implants and convinced myself I was doing it for me. I made up some flimsy excuse that I was doing it to balance my chest to my larger rear end. I always thought my butt was too big and stuck out way too far. I also didn't like my thighs. I wanted really thin thighs as opposed to the shapely, muscular legs that I actually have. I thought that by "balancing out" my figure I would finally be happy with myself. What I really wanted, though, was approval and external validation from men.

Flash-forward, and now I am fifty-three. I lift weights, I have run half-marathons, and I am halfway to a black belt in Krav Maga. My body is strong and healthy, and I just recently started to love and appreciate it. Seriously, I actually love my body at fifty-three more than I did at twenty. That is because I have the maturity and life perspective to appreciate all the things about it that are unique. I love my body not only for its unique beauty but for its strength. I appreciate it for all it has endured – residency, childbirth, and cancer – all of which really took a toll. The resilience of my body completely amazes me. I now know that my body doesn't exist to please men. It serves as a vehicle for me to experience the world.

Scars

That appreciation allowed me to make a powerful decision – to have my implants removed. Over the past few years, I have noticed how much large breasts get in the way of every activity. I have been plagued with pain and discomfort, especially in my left breast. All tests have been normal, but things just don't feel right. Then a friend brought BII (breast implant illness) to my attention. Apparently, there is a community of women who are plagued by vague symptoms only to have them resolved once the implants were removed.

I decided that even if none of these symptoms resolve, the implants were a foreign body. An invader from the shell of the person I used to be. I decided to get an explant and a lift. During the months before my surgery, I imagined myself with smaller breasts and wondered if I would be happy with the outcome. When the surgery day arrived, I decided I would be happy with the outcome as long as I was healthy.

That first breath of air, feeling my lungs expand fully without that weight on my chest felt amazing. A literal and figurative weight had been removed. The implants carried emotional baggage and scars from my old life. Still, I thought, "What if I don't feel like a woman without larger breasts?" To my surprise, on the day of the unveiling, when the bandages were removed, I was elated. Beyond the drains, bandages, and surgical incisions was the real me. My body looked amazing. I was used to looking at my breasts, but now I could see my waist, the curves of my hips, and my thighs, and what I felt like was the perfect proportion. It's amazing that it takes us women so long to appreciate our own bodies. It's sad that we let men and society dictate what beauty is. Beauty doesn't fit a mold. It is present in everyone and everything, but many of us choose not to see it.

Renewal

> THE WAY YOU LOOK SHOULD BE A REFLECTION OF HOW YOU FEEL ON THE INSIDE, NOT A REFLECTION OF SOMEONE ELSE.

A few years after my cancer diagnosis, after I had gotten back into the rhythm of life, I started to think about myself. My health. My body. My emotional wellness. After dealing with cancer, I wanted to treat all of me better. I actually needed to make myself a priority. I started paying more attention to my eating and exercising regimens. But that wasn't enough. My skin was lacking radiance. I had dark spots, and the texture was terrible. I wasn't surprised, since my beauty regimen for most of my life consisted of soap and water. I started to use the medical-grade products I had in my medspa, hoping for a quick improvement. Instead, my skin was red, itchy, and flaky. This was not my desired outcome, but since they were medical-grade products I thought they were good for me. I tried to research the ingredients, but they were nowhere to be found. They were not on the bottle and not available online. *Why is that,* I thought? Why would medical-grade products not flaunt the amazing ingredients? Then I started to put it all together. Itching, flaking, redness, and ingredients that were difficult to find information on. Perhaps the products weren't as good for me as I may have thought? After more digging, I found out I was right.

At first, the realization didn't affect me greatly. Then, after following my beauty routine as usual, I bolted out of bed in the middle of the night feeling an intense desire to scrub my face to get rid of any toxins. So, I did exactly that. I wondered why on earth I would compromise safety for the sake of beauty. I felt like that compromise wasn't necessary. There was clearly a void in the market for consumers. I no longer felt good about selling these products to my clients, so, the next morning, I threw thousands of dollars of inventory into the trash.

What I found was there are basically four kinds of products in the market. The drugstore brands are the most easily accessible and affordable. They are mass-produced, and consumers recognize the names. What consumers don't know is that these products are filled with chemicals and don't have quality active ingredients.

Salon-grade products are sold in salons. They have a higher price tag and are often well-known brands, but many of them have the same issues as drugstore brands.

Physician-formulated skincare products make consumers feel better because they are backed by a physician. It is important to understand that physician-formulated skin care will be formulated based on the personal philosophy of that physician. That is why it is important to check the ingredients carefully to make sure you are comfortable with them. I personally review ingredient profiles very carefully with all my personal care products.

I found this was the case with the popular brand I sold in my spa. It worked well initially but later left my skin feeling violated. Many of these products are celebrity-endorsed or are part of a multilevel marketing platform. This is a strategy that direct sales companies use where existing distributors are paid a percentage of their recruits' sales. It is often great for the company as it can yield rapid growth with minimal advertising. Yet, for the consumer, skincare sales are made by people with no skincare knowledge or expertise other than what is given to them by the company. Additionally, the primary incentive becomes money, not skin health, since there is a low cost of entry for the distributors.

High-end department store brands also occupy some market space and are sometimes more expensive than medical-grade skincare lines. They have a boutique feel with attractive packaging and luxurious aromas. Many work well, but in my opinion the quality doesn't justify the expense.

In the past few years, "natural" products have started to occupy more of the marketplace as consumers become more savvy about ingredients and their health. If you really look at the ingredient deck, the first few may be natural, like shea butter or avocado, but once you look deeper, they still contain many chemicals.

After learning all of this, it left me feeling that the skincare industry could do better. It should be held to higher standards. I wanted products that were effective and did not contain ingredients that didn't nourish the skin. Products with plant-based, active ingredients that were cruelty-free and vegan-friendly.

So, I did more research. I found another physician-formulated skincare line in a local organic foods store. I thought about taking the easy way out and retailing this product in my spa. But there were so many choices, and it was difficult to figure out what product to use for what skin concerns. People want simple and straightforward skincare they don't need to think about. As I tested the product, I realized I didn't like the packaging or the putrid clinical aroma. The products also left behind a residue.

I wondered if I could create a product line with effective active ingredients, no toxic chemicals, no residue or harsh odors, AND attractive packaging.

That's when my next mission became clear. I thought this was a way to realize my childhood dream of helping millions of people. I would use my medical knowledge to create a line of skincare products that would be good for all skin types and pigments and would work for all ages. My avenue to empower women to feel confident through beauty. To help them develop the courage to listen to their inner voices and create better lives.

Chapter 10

SEXISM & RACISM

BEING A MOTHER DOES NOT MEAN YOU HAVE TO BE A MARTYR.

Being a woman is hard enough, but being the type of woman I am was even more difficult. I didn't conform to the accepted female archetype. Most women I knew looked to become someone's wife and mother. They also subscribed to the theory that Motherhood=Martyrdom. I am a caring and nurturing person, but the idea of being a martyr makes me vomit a little. Yes, I can cook, clean, and do all kinds of domestic chores, but I don't like them one bit. I would rather be in my office because that is my happy place. Somehow, I was made to feel guilty for working all my life because I didn't fit the traditional role of mother. There is no predefined role for surgeon mom. This meant I didn't volunteer, make my kids' lunches, clean their messes, or do their laundry once they were old enough to handle these things themselves. I definitely did not bake cookies or host play dates because I was at work. I spent quality time with my children every evening that I wasn't on call. I talked and laughed with them instead of being their maid. Nor did I worry about keeping them busy every second of the day. This meant that instead of feeling like I couldn't wait to get rid of them, they were my salvation from work at the end of the day. Let's be honest: I did want to get rid of them some of the time.

Society is still stuck in 1950 on this subject. Men work, and the "wifeys" stay home to cook, clean, and raise children. Many of these women are forced to give up their careers and autonomy because their husbands outearn them. After losing their autonomy and their personal power, they subsequently feel they have no value in the home. They are last, their families are first. Is this what we should be teaching our daughters? That they have no value and should be last? That their desires and needs are unworthy of attention? Yet, this is what society claims is correct. If we raise sons, we show them that women are worthless and all men's needs should be first.

In Ancient Egypt, it wasn't uncommon for women to rule. Of course, we all know Cleopatra, who ruled Egypt in 51–30 B.C. How is it that, in 2022, women are condemned to be inferior when centuries ago they ruled. When did we allow this? As the mother of two sons, this was the last thing I wanted to show them. I didn't want them to treat any woman (especially me) as if they had no value. So, I did things differently. I made sure my sons realized that their mother was not their own personal servant.

The interesting thing is that, even when women are the primary breadwinners in their families, they are still expected to do the lion's share of the household duties and often allow their husbands to be the final say in financial decisions. I am ashamed to admit that I did this, too. As of 2019, thirty-eight percent of women outearned their spouses, and there is no doubt that this number will continue to increase.

Sexism in the workplace is another issue. I was never part of the "all boys club" the other male doctors belonged to. How could I be?

I didn't flirt inappropriately with nurses at the hospital or play golf on the weekends. It turns out not having a penis is a serious business disadvantage because referrals from other doctors were based on camaraderie, not skill or merit. My medical decisions were second-guessed until a male physician agreed with the plan of care.

This was nothing new. In medical school and residency, I faced dual discrimination: being a female in a male-dominated field and being a person of color.

Sexual harassment was also a problem. During my residency, even though I was married, the other residents were very flirtatious. Then, during my general surgery year, one surgeon I rotated with would try to touch me inappropriately in the operating room and say inappropriate things to me. At first, I wasn't going to say anything because, as the only female in the residency, I didn't want to be "that girl." It got to the point, though, where I couldn't take it anymore. I hated the fact that he was going to get away with this behavior, so I had to do something. I went to the program director, not knowing if he would be supportive or not. Surprisingly, he placed me with a different doctor and reprimanded the surgeon.

WOMEN TEND NOT TO SPEAK UP FOR FEAR THAT THEY WILL APPEAR WEAK. REAL STRENGTH IS REQUIRED TO SPEAK UP FOR YOUR NEEDS.

There were other instances where I didn't speak up for myself so I wouldn't be thought of as less competent than a man. Sexism in the workplace stifled my judgment and ability to speak up, take care of myself, and take care of my unborn child. Although I was healthy, I went into preterm labor twice due to grueling hours of residency and limited nourishment and hydration. I was on call after working a twelve-hour day. I started to experience significant back pain. The nurses were concerned, but I ignored them and went about my business. The leaking amniotic fluid (which I originally thought was urine) finally got my attention. I called my doctor, who urged me to meet him at the hospital right away.

I felt guilty leaving, so the nurses took over, called in another resident, and sent me on my way. I called my husband en route to the hospital. What I wanted to say was, "I really need you there because I am so worried and scared." What came out of my mouth, though, was, "You don't need to meet me because I am sure everything is fine. I will be in and out of there in an hour." Again, I refused to show vulnerability or that I needed support. Thank God he didn't listen, because our first son, Roland, was born that day six weeks earlier than expected. His lungs weren't fully developed despite the steroid shot I received, and he wound up on a ventilator for twenty-four hours. It was the most horrific and wonderful day of my life. I was thrilled to meet my son but devastated that I failed as a mother to keep him safe in utero for the time period he needed to be in there. Now he was fighting against a world he wasn't ready for at a weight of four pounds six ounces.

With my younger son, I had some warning. For weeks, I had a recurring dream that I went into preterm labor and didn't have a hospital bag packed. After about two weeks, I went ahead and packed a bag just so the dream would stop. A few days later, right before a long surgery, I started having back pain. This time I called my doctor immediately and confidently left the hospital knowing that I was doing the right thing for my unborn child. Luckily, I was admitted to the hospital and given medications to stop the labor. I went home on bedrest for the rest of my pregnancy. My second son, Derek, was delivered at thirty-eight weeks and thankfully had no health issues.

Going back to work was an emotional roller coaster. I felt judged by everyone. I listened to the tone in everyone's voice when I said I was leaving my children in daycare and going back to work. People would ask if I felt guilty. They would ask how I could possibly leave a small baby at a daycare with strangers. Why don't people ask a new father the same questions? And I really had no choice. I spent fifteen years training for my profession and hundreds of thousands of dollars; I couldn't afford NOT to go back to work. Because I hadn't made peace with my own desire to work, I allowed the opinions of others to infect me. It was a double-edged sword; I missed my children when I wasn't with them, but I missed work when I wasn't at work. No matter how cute they were, baby talk, feedings, and diaper changes weren't enough to keep me mentally challenged. Each woman has a right to choose her path to fulfillment.

Once my sons were born, I tried to breastfeed as much as I could. One time, I was the chief surgeon on a total laryngectomy and bilateral neck dissection. Basically, this is a very long and complicated surgery, and we started the operation at five p.m. After about six hours, my breasts were so engorged that it hurt to move my arms. I hated to excuse myself, but I just had to. If I didn't, breast milk would literally pour out on its own. I will never forget the look on the attending surgeon's face when I said I need to be excused. He said, "Why?" "I need to pump," I responded. I was getting better at speaking up, but it still frightened me.

There were so many issues that the male residents didn't have to deal with. They didn't have to operate sideways because of a large belly or pump breast milk while on call or operating. They usually had wives or girlfriends to take care of children and everything for them at home.

Starting a practice as a female surgeon was also agonizing in some respects. Everybody would assume I was the nurse and ask, "Where's the doctor? We thought you'd be a man. You're just so young." That kind of thing. Apparently taking care of oneself is a career detriment. One patient in my practice said, "I'm sorry, but I really don't feel comfortable because you're a woman and you're too young." Funny thing is, the doctor he wound up going to, while a man, was about a year younger than I was. But that doctor was bald, so maybe he just looked more the part. I guess my appearance bound me to society's belief that I couldn't be both competent and attractive. Skill and professionalism should extend far beyond superficial appearance.

St. Augustine, Florida, where I practice, is an old, old city. In fact, it's the oldest continuously populated city in the United States. You would think that a city that's been around this long would be more broadminded and avant-garde than it is, but it really isn't. Some people are closed-minded and old-fashioned.

We chose St. Augustine to live in when I was finishing up my residency in Philadelphia. A colleague who worked part-time in St. Augustine said it was a great place in which to practice. We were familiar with it since my in-laws lived there. Sadly enough, one of the local physicians had passed away, and there was a real need for an ENT. But I wasn't welcomed with open arms in any way.

One of the doctors was older and did things the old-fashioned way. I knew there would be challenges working together. The only other doctor told me straight out, "We don't need another ENT here. There's no need for you to come."

Welcome to St. Augustine

So, I decided to start my own practice while simultaneously second-guessing my decision to move to this town. Rejection is tough, but adversity often brings out the true character in a person. I was not going to quit. People, for the most part, don't like change. Most people like to stay in their comfort zones. I had to figure out how I offered something different. I offered a different style. I had a conversational approach with my patients, outlining options and helping them decide what was best for them. Most physicians treated medicine as a dictatorship.

Being a female business owner is like beginning a race way behind the starting line, where everyone is right at the line and others get a significant head start. A woman is behind the ball simply because she's a woman and not privy to the "good ol' boys" network. Doubly so if you're a woman of color, which puts your starting position much, much further back. This kind of systemic discrimination unfortunately still exists everywhere – but in the South, it's especially prevalent. So much so that it's a way of life to continue the disparity.

Many of these men grew up together, and their families have known each other for generations, so breaking through boundaries becomes a major part of daily life.

As women, we have the opportunity and the right to choose how to live. We can choose to stay home and raise our children or go to work and have our husbands stay home. We can choose not to have children. We can choose not to have a career. We can choose who we want our romantic partners to be.

We should not feel guilty for our choices, nor do we have to explain them to others. Each family should do things the way that works best for all members of the family to thrive, not just survive.

As women, we have been underestimated for decades and have bought into the lie that we aren't as capable as our male counterparts, and we have, in many cases, willingly relinquished our own power. Without our personal power, we lose our self-esteem, our independence, and our voice. We do not maintain healthy boundaries and therefore become martyrs for everyone else's happiness instead of champions for our own happiness and success.

Chapter 11

FINDING AUTHENTICITY

Finding My Name

Shakespeare wrote, "That which we call a rose, by any other name would smell as sweet." I disagree. I believe names and identities are our first impressions to the world about who we are. Names represent how we feel about ourselves. I knew this because after being called a bitch enough times I believed it. My last name embraced an Italian heritage that was not mine. I had taken my husband's last name in marriage because it was tradition, and I didn't want to be seen as one of those crazy "feminist" types that either hyphenated her name or, worse, kept her maiden name that everyone made fun of. I also bought into the theory that my whole family should have the same last name. Mostly because I wanted it to be easier for when I had children. I had the thoughts that everyone does: *If I had a different last name, how would anyone know I was their mother? And how would everyone know I was my husband's wife?* So, instead of making things difficult for everyone else, I chose to have my identity confirmed by signifying that I belonged to my husband.

I have a friend who actually had her husband take HER last name – and that was almost twenty years ago. I thought she was crazy at the time, but now she is my hero! I recently asked her how she and her husband came to that agreement. She is a physician licensed in many states, and he was a nurse. He had a complicated upbringing and therefore had no attachment to his last name. He asked if he could take her name because he felt her family was like his own. This story was refreshing to me. After all, marriage should be a merger, not a takeover. Each couple should have the freedom to write their story the way they see fit.

RECLAIMING MY MAIDEN NAME WAS A BIG STEP TO RECLAIMING MYSELF.

My maiden name, Sundar, is the Indian word for beauty. Welcoming my maiden name back was a big step toward accepting and being proud of my color, heritage, freedom, spirit, and individuality. It felt like revisiting the part of me that got lost over the years and reconnecting with her. I wanted to reconnect with the free-spirited dreamer. I wanted to reconnect with her before everyone and society tamed her and beat the fight out of her. I wanted to reclaim and repossess her in her raw form. I am her, and she is me. She was never gone, just buried and forgotten.

With that realization, I changed back to my maiden name. Taking back my last name, Sundar portrays my transition into becoming Unbound.

Finding My Path

Everyone has opinions about what you should do. From the important decisions, such as your career and raising your children and who you date, to the trivial things like what you should wear and how you should act. After my divorce, I polled everyone about my life's choices and came up with so many different opinions. We ask others because we don't trust ourselves. We have become untrained to listen to that inner voice, the voice that knows deep inside of us.

> WE TEND TO RELY ON OTHER OPINIONS WHEN WE CAN'T HEAR OUR INNER VOICE.

Hearing that voice amidst the noise isn't easy. I learned to hear it by meditating. At first, I heard nothing, but as I continued, I was able to hear more and get answers more quickly. The consistency now brings me clear answers even when I am not meditating. Meditation has become an important and consistent practice in my life.

As I started shifting my career path, I made the mistake of asking others what they thought. When asking others, you will often get the safe and conformist answer. It was unanimous: *I was a good doctor, and I should stay in medicine. It was a safe and comfortable life. So many years in training…blah, blah blah.* Why didn't anyone care that I was unhappy and that I had suicidal thoughts regularly? Why wasn't being fulfilled in your career choice important? Yes, I realized my decision was risky, but sometimes the greatest risks come with the greatest rewards. I have always loved starting and building businesses. And I have always been successful. My new career path involved combining this passion with the knowledge and experience I had from two decades in medicine. I would be able to utilize my skills in media to market the new business.

I had also foolishly mentioned to a few of my friends that I was considering a divorce, and that brought out quite a bit of resistance. If everything was mediocre, why would I consider a divorce? *If it isn't broken, you don't need to fix it…blah, blah, blah.* For them, it was always about surviving and being in a comfort zone, not about flourishing and living your best life. I was shocked at how many people had this mentality. It was clear that not only did I need a new life, I needed some new damn friends. I needed to be in the company of people who would be a bit bolder and more audacious.

Finding My Voice

OUR VOICE AND WORDS CREATE A PATH TO AUTHENTICITY.

I identify with Ariel from *The Little Mermaid* because, after stifling my voice for so many years, singing became a way for me to express myself. When I first started, I could barely be heard. I had trouble increasing the volume of my voice. After all, I had been conditioned that my voice wasn't supposed to be heard. The voice that came out of my mouth was weak, pitchy, and fabricated. Just like me and my life. I hoped to eventually hear my real voice come through in my singing. I knew my real voice would emerge alongside the real authentic me. My voice was weak and breathy because there was tension in my throat. I was embarrassed and shy and lacked confidence when it came to showing this vulnerable side of myself. I was afraid I wasn't good enough. I was judging myself and afraid to be judged by others.

As a child, I sang all the time. My mother grew up singing in India and was a sought-after vocalist for events. She has an amazing voice. We would sing together. I sang songs in multiple languages. I loved to sing and was confident and assured. I have listened to the tapes (yes, cassette tapes) of me singing at the age of two. I wondered why I was so different now. Every time I opened my mouth to sing, I had a flashback to the last time I sang.

I was on stage in India and wanted to sing "You Light Up My Life" by Debby Boone – my favorite song at the time. It was 1977. The event was one that my uncle had put together. The room was full of seventy-five people that I knew well. I was excited to sing, but I had never used a microphone before. As I started, my song sounded terrible. There was feedback and screeching, but I kept singing, trying desperately to fix my performance. When I was done, everyone clapped enthusiastically to be polite. I even won first place, but I didn't deserve it.

I barely remember how it felt that night, but my body does. I immediately feel unworthy to be on stage and not good enough. My vocal cords constrict, and my neck muscles tighten. I feel like I can't fill my lungs with enough air. I am critical about every note that escapes my mouth. The irony in this is that your best voice comes out of you when you are most relaxed and free. Not when you feel like someone is strangling you. That was going to be the challenge for sure. Sing? I knew I could sing. The challenge was fixing the crap in my head.

I needed to maintain control while being free. And I needed to use proper breath support and control the way I articulate the words and the quality of my tone to express different "color" and emotions. Yes, all this while feeling FREE. The more things I was told to pay attention to, the more my throat closed. I was forced to sing things I didn't like, so my singing got worse. Basically, I quit singing for a long damn time. I quit until Martin walked into my life.

Martin was a nineteen-year-old hipster I contacted to teach my oldest son how to sing. He showed up an hour late for the first lesson. His hair was all over the place in a mess of unruly curls. I questioned the last time he even showered because he was in his bathing suit. I thought, "This isn't going to work out at all."

Then he sat down and played the piano, and I watched how he interacted with my son. They were like long lost friends talking about what kind of music they liked. They sang a song together, and Martin played it better than the version I heard on the radio. As I escorted him to the door, he politely asked me if I was interested in setting up another lesson. I asked him if he would be my vocal coach, and I was excited that he coached women.

As I started to take lessons from Martin, I realized that getting taught by a musician was indeed different from taking lessons from a music teacher. He taught in an unconventional way and made it fun. I learned that there were certain songs more suitable for my voice. I recognized that I felt more free with a teacher who could change things up into a slightly different key or melody. In all those years of conventional piano and voice lessons, the missing element was creativity. I was so focused on the perfection of each note and the perfect execution of Beethoven's "Für Elise" on piano that I missed something important.

WE OFTEN STRIVE FOR PERFECTION NOT RECOGNIZING THAT OUR IMPERFECTIONS ADD DEPTH AND CHARACTER.

Just like my perfect life, perfect pitch, perfect execution of each note, and perfectly played musical performances lack a certain character. They lack the beauty of imperfection that adds quality and depth to music and life. The same is true of beauty. Beauty lies not in perfection but the harmony and balance of the seemingly imperfect parts of the face.

For years, I wanted to create my own music. I would sit at the piano and not know what to do. My intention was to sit down and create some masterpiece, but it doesn't work that way. So, instead, I sat down and fiddled around with keys. Some combinations were good. Others were terrible. I got an idea of what sounds I liked and disliked. I took songs I could play on the piano and sing. I changed them a bit. I kept doing these things until one day some inspiration hit. I had some lyrics scrolling through my head during my drive home. I immediately wrote them down on paper and surprisingly wrote my first song. For some reason, I didn't care what anyone thought about the song. I liked it, and it meant something to me. I sang "Force of Nature" at my fiftieth birthday party as my friend, John, rocked the guitar. One of my girlfriends grabbed me immediately after and said, "Wow – I've never heard you sing like that before. You were singing from your heart!" And she was right. For the first time in my life, I was singing freely. I wasn't doing it to impress or win anyone's approval. I sang lyrics from my heart with the voice that radiated from the depths of my soul. It was one of my truest moments in life.

I now have close friendships that stemmed from our mutual love of music. I sing with my older son, and that is a special connection. My brother and I both sing, and he plays the guitar. We joke about having our own show just like Donny and Marie. Music added a different depth to our relationship and helped me unlock one of the chains that was binding me.

It made me realize that sometimes there are things in our lives that we know are important but don't make time to do because they don't help us "advance" in the game of life. But exploring music and singing has opened up so many new connections and doors for me.

Chapter 12

SMASHING THE STATUS QUO

Intuition

Intuition is a word we all use, but many of us don't even know what it means. Intuition is the ability to understand something immediately without the need for conscious reasoning.

I believe all of us have intuition, but many of us choose not to listen to it. In any case, it's there with very useful information. Until we decide it serves no purpose. I have been trained all my life to use logic and reason to make my decisions. But logic seems to have failed me thus far. Logic would have had me stay in my marriage and continue on the career path I chose at the age of five. Logic completely led me astray. Logic and intuition are at war with one another deep within my psyche. Logic fuels my lies, and intuition ignites my truth. Lies are always easier to digest. Lies are woven from what you want to hear. The truth hurts, spits in your face, and is harsh. The truth is unrelenting and won't go away no matter how you try to hide it. That's what intuition is. You can bury it, but it will resurface. You can hide it, but it will become revealed. You can ignore it, but it won't go away until you listen.

I don't fight it anymore. I succumb. I let the intuition absorb and guide me. Intuition leads me to my truest path and never leads me astray. When logic tries to persuade me to go in a different direction, I spit in its face and tell it to go to hell.

When my gut speaks, it speaks the truth. I know it from the feeling that bubbles deep inside me. I feel the bubbling often, as it is my cue to tune in. Once I listen, answers become clear. When logic speaks, the answers are not clear – they are confusing. The answers are convoluted. That's how I know the difference.

The Love I Shouldn't Give Myself

I look in the mirror every day. To see if my hair is sticking up, whether I have food in my teeth, to see if I look fat…I do the front view, side view, and back view before I leave the house. I even look in the mirror several times a day, checking this or that. But one day my friend told me to really look into my eyes in the mirror and tell myself that I love me.

When I feel love, I have no problem saying it to someone. I told my husband, children, and friends that I love them often. So how hard could this really be? I decided to get to it after polishing off two glasses of wine during a virtual happy hour with Elisa during COVID. Virtual meetings, work, happy hours, and even virtual sex at times. Hell – why not? It's safer.

I confidently strutted up to the mirror, ready to do this. Then I looked into my eyes. I didn't even recognize the eyes staring back at me. Because I have never looked into my own eyes like that. In my own eyes I saw uncertainty, power, pride, and self-doubt. Mostly, I saw the real me, the one that's been locked away being protected by the "tough me." You see, the tough me – let's call her Tough Tessa – doesn't allow the real me to surface. Tough Tessa doesn't think Kalpana could handle any pain, so she kept me safe. And she was right, until now. We can't avoid pain. It is necessary to grow, to heal, and to truly understand joy. Without pain, you can't truly appreciate joy. As human beings, we are hardwired to avoid pain. If you put your hand in a fire, you will instinctively pull your hand out. We have to move past our instincts of pain avoidance and calmly learn to embrace pain. We need to feel it all, not drown it in drugs, alcohol, or some other addiction. Every bit of pain I have encountered has taught me, changed me, and improved me to become the person I am today. And I know it's not over, as there is a hell of a lot more pain to come. With it will come a new version of me. Better than the one before.

When I looked in the mirror, I shoved Tough Tessa out of the way and let the real me look back. My eyes no longer had that tough stare. They were milky brown and warm. I opened my mouth to say "I love you" as I stared at my reflection, but the words wouldn't come out. What came out instead were sobs and tears. Why was it so hard to look myself in the eyes and say this? I regained my composure and just did it. "I love you," I said. "I love you for all of you, your greatness, your imperfections, and everything. I love you unconditionally no matter what!"

The sobbing continued, but I vowed I would look in the mirror every day and say this to myself until I could do it without crying. It took ten days. I challenge all of you to look at yourself in the mirror. It will challenge you and what you think of yourself.

It starts with self-love, but this will fuel self-esteem and proper boundary development. Then we start to realize we can actually be pretty self-sufficient.

EVERY WOMAN NEEDS
A GIRLFRIEND WHO SEES
IN YOU WHAT YOU CAN'T
SEE IN YOURSELF – YET!

One of the best things a woman can have during this self-love learning period is a friend who loves you more than you love yourself.

During the period where I couldn't love myself completely, Nancy would remind me how awesome I am. Because somewhere deep inside, that hurt little girl who couldn't get her father's attention was still aching. The good news is that she ached less and less every day that she validated herself. Every day she required less validation from others. Until the day came where she decided she was pretty fucking awesome. She has been pretending she knew she was awesome for fifty years, but she finally believed it at fifty years and six months.

Nancy and I had "counseling sessions" every morning. We were the first texts to each other every day. We joked and said we needed boyfriends who were as amazing to us as we were to each other. And that's where we set the bar. After all, we accepted each other even though we had our differences, and we loved each other unconditionally. We would jokingly say that we only NEED a man for "one thing." Truth be told, she has said repeatedly that we would have the perfect relationship if only she could grow a penis!

It turns out you don't even really need a man for that one thing. Want, yes – need, no. I will have to admit, there was a part of me that really wanted to be in a relationship so I could have regular sex. But here is the silver lining: the lack of regular (aka, possibly very boring vanilla) sex leads one to experimentation. You see, self-love can include sex. I learned quite a lot about my likes and dislikes during this period. I learned all about my erogenous zones, toys, what I liked and disliked. This allowed for much better sex since I knew what I wanted and had time to experiment.

WE NEED TO LOVE THE
PARTS OF OURSELVES
THAT ARE HARD TO LOVE.

Self-love really hides behind a bunch of fake security blankets. We all have them. I had a lot of them. I only loved myself…if I was successful, if I was fit, if my boobs were the right size, if my hair was long, and if I was making the right amount of money. All examples of conditional love. Sometimes I would be doing so great with self-love and then, lo and behold, a giant pimple would erupt on my forehead and that self-love would immediately turn into self-loathing. It's amazing how one single blemish can take us over the edge. I decided to shed each of my attachments to these conditions and allowed myself to be loved.

Since I was already successful, I decided to love myself because I was kind, not because of success. I had surgery to remove my breast implants for the sake of my health, even if it left me with a B cup and a scar. To my surprise, I never regretted having my small breasts back. I knew the scars would fade, but I would always remember that I altered my body because I didn't love myself enough to leave it alone. I even gained a bit of weight and got a bit "squishy" after surgery since I couldn't exercise much for six weeks. Instead of self-loathing in the mirror, I was grateful for the new, healthy me without the toxic implants. A few weeks after my surgery, I chopped off my long hair and replaced it with a shorter, sassier cut. It felt good to shed the layers of the old me. During all of this, I was fortunate enough to not have any unsightly blemishes.

The Dog I Didn't Think I Wanted

I have a distant memory of being with my parents and seeing an adorable small dog. He was playful and friendly, and I could tell he really liked me. I bugged my parents for a dog, but they didn't want one. They were too much work and too much trouble. Ironically, once I left for college, my mom got a dog, and she was very attached to him. So attached that she almost didn't make it to my engagement party because she couldn't find someone to watch him. I hate to admit it, but I resented that dog. A LOT. Not only was he a constant reminder of the dog I never got to have, but now he had all of my mom's attention. He was clearly more important than me. That was when I decided I never wanted a dog. I assumed that once I had a dog I would not appreciate human interaction as much as interaction with the dog. I have heard people say that they like their dog more than they like people, and I didn't want to be one of those people.

One of my best friends, Stacy, is a veterinarian, and we have known each other since college. Recently, since my divorce, I would call or text Stacy about random pet ideas because dogs were too much work. "Should I get a monkey?" "No!" she would say. "An iguana?" "Sure, if that's what you want," she would say while warning me that an iguana may not give me the satisfaction that I want from a pet. "Well, that may be true, but I don't have to feed it much, listen to it bark, potty train it, or have it eat my shoes!" There was a long pause on the other end of the phone. That's when she said, "Kal, get a cactus, for heaven's sake!"

I continued to tell everyone how I never wanted a dog. Until one day I started seriously thinking about getting a puppy. I started thinking about it right after my divorce but knew better than to make such a drastic decision. So, I waited a few years to see what my new life would be like and if a dog would fit into it. I knew what characteristics I was looking for in a puppy but didn't know if this kind of puppy actually existed.

One day, Stacy made the bold leap and told me about this adorable puppy that she checked out. She felt he had the perfect temperament for me and could fit into my life. I really don't believe in love at first sight, but in this case, that was what happened. I looked at his little face and decided that somehow I would figure out how to take care of him. I put him in my lap and took him home. I named him Enzo – after Enzo Ferrari – because I like fast cars and good-looking Italian men. And because I fell in love with Enzo, the dog in *The Art of Racing in the Rain*. That first day, when we drove home, he sat in my lap and looked up at me with his big brown eyes. I melted. He adjusted himself accordingly as I shifted gears, and my driving soothed him. Yes, this dog was made for me. He was the perfect little companion.

THE UNCONDITIONAL LOVE FROM A PET CAN MELT ANY HEART.

What happened over the next few months was even more surprising. Enzo managed to melt away my tough, icy exterior, revealing some fluffy marshmallow interior I didn't even know existed. I was playful and acted ridiculously with this dog. The child I never got to be was emerging. My relationship with my younger son even improved after Enzo came into my life. He said, "Mom, you are so much softer and nicer since you got Enzo." I pondered that for a long time. I have been hiding behind a tough exterior for so long that I didn't know the real me.

When I told Stacy what my son said, she said, "Enzo fixes everything." And just maybe he did. Life after Enzo is different. I am softer and kinder, but I still have boundaries. Apparently, you don't have to be an Ice Queen so that people don't take advantage of you. You can be kind and loving AND maintain healthy boundaries. I am thrilled that I learned this at fifty instead of seventy.

The Tattoo I Should Never Get

"You don't put a bumper sticker on a Ferrari," I would say. I wasn't a fan of tattoos, nor was I ever going to get one. But after seeing Adam Levine, the lead singer of Maroon 5, covered in tattoos, I fell in love. With him and his tattoos. Like a lovesick teenager, I attended a bunch of concerts back to back not being able to get enough of him. Suddenly, tattoos I thought were hideous were insanely sexy!

As I started meditating, journaling, and taking time to reflect, I believed there was something to be said for my getting thyroid cancer, a disease centered in the fifth chakra of the neck, and me being bound to the choices and opinions of others. I realize that not everybody believes in the concept of chakras, but if you know anything about them, you know there are seven. The first three are chakras of basic needs, creativity and sexuality, and personal power. The fourth chakra is the connection between matter and spirit, like love and connection. The last three are the chakras of spirit, like verbal expression and the ability to speak our highest truth, intuition, and enlightenment.

My fifth chakra was obviously the problem. The way I was living my life was blocking it. I was holding myself back from being the best version of myself and living life to the fullest. I was living in fear. Fear of disappointing others, fear that others wouldn't understand, and fear that they wouldn't love me for living my life as I wanted. I was killing myself doing work I no longer enjoyed. I was living with a man who was no longer heading where I wanted my life to go. I was living in a place where I never fit in. I knew it was time to make some bold changes, but I didn't make the changes right away. Needless to say, it took years after this encounter for me to make the changes.

To commemorate this bold revelation and my journey to becoming unbound, I got ink. Many people get tattoos while inebriated, putting no thought into what they permanently imprint on their bodies. I got my first tattoo at forty-nine after thinking about it for almost ten years.

The Career I Could Never Have

It was the spring of 1976 or so. My class took a school trip to the local television station in New York City. The air was crisp, and the sun kept us warm as we walked there. We were all talking about the movie *Freaky Friday*. I hadn't seen it yet and was dying to. We were going to experience what went on behind the cameras and have an opportunity to be filmed. I remember that day vividly, which is strange because I can't say that about most of my childhood. It was hot and a little humid. I was wearing this light green and yellow, leafy print dress. My class was walking down this long and winding hallway, then we waited in line for our turn to be filmed. Everyone was saying how much they didn't like this field trip. They wanted to be in Central Park. Mostly, they were saying how nervous they were about being filmed.

> WE OFTEN HEAR THE TRUE CALLING OF THE SOUL AS CHILDREN. SUPPRESSING THAT CALLING IS LEARNED BEHAVIOR.

I was the only one who felt the opposite. Being filmed was a totally different experience for me. I loved seeing myself on camera, and I remember thinking, *I wonder if this is what I could do with my life? Do something on TV.* There were so many more people I could reach than I could as a doctor. I wanted so much to tell my parents about the experience and how I felt, but I couldn't, especially after I'd already told them about wanting to be a doctor. Somehow, I knew changing my path to television from medicine would not go over well. So, I told myself I wasn't going to say anything. And I didn't. I just told them I went on a field trip.

There's a distinct difference between finding a path to take and entering the freeway of the soul. In a way, I found my path in life by accident. I was so young. I had no idea of my propensity for science, I just knew I wanted to help heal someone I loved. The best way to do that, in my mind, was to become a doctor. My parents' positive reaction, especially my father's, supported my decision. As I thought about my choice, I realized I could potentially help not only my father, but hundreds, maybe thousands, of others. I liked that idea. I instinctively knew the path was right. It made sense in my mind.

But when I saw myself on television, something deeper awakened inside of me. That excitement emanated from my soul. I instinctively felt the change of direction and the whole experience imprinted on my soul. I didn't know how I could use a medium like television in my future. I just knew I would be good at it, and I had proven it when

I saw myself on television. I glimpsed at the entrance to my soul's freeway, but, like most girls, I passed it by because I had already found a path that would please others immensely. Please myself to some degree, but mostly please others.

What I didn't realize was that I was teaching myself to be inauthentic. I was teaching myself to look to others for approval and acceptance when I should possibly have found the courage to tell my parents about my experience. In both scenarios, my instincts were correct. It's just that I got directions for one road externally and the other internally.

I learned early to ignore my sense of knowing and doubt my instincts. Most of us get bound in this way around the age of ten. I was no exception. I continued to live bound to other people's opinions and desires for my life. Later, and a long way down my path, my instincts found a way to take over and wake me up to the truth that my life needed to change. Immediately.

We end up making career decisions to impress other people so we can feel that fleeting rush of validation. In the process, we lose sight of what makes us truly happy. With each career move, we get unhappier. The more we try to impress, the more frustrated we feel. We notice our neighbors have better cars than we do, we see that our cousins or sisters or friends are doing well, and we try to make our careers match or exceed their perceived level of impressiveness. This only leads to future dissatisfaction despite how much money we make.

Many of us choose a career before we really know and understand ourselves and what brings us joy. That said, many of us have invested a lot of time and money in a career choice. Perhaps there is a way to combine or utilize your current career and combine it with other talents? What if we are open to the possibility of a career change at whatever point true inspiration comes to us? For me, it took almost five decades. Better late than never, right?

The Time We Should Never "Waste"

Some of your greatest joys and creative moments come to you when you are unproductive. As women, we put pressure on ourselves. Society places pressure on us. During this pandemic, I had more time than I have ever had in my life. Time to think, time to breathe, time to just be. I used to feel good about myself only when I accomplished something and felt like a failure when I didn't get everything done on my to-do list.

But now, since the COVID-19 pandemic, I take pleasure in sitting idle, thinking, petting my dog, and listening to him purr. (Yes, he purrs. It's the craziest thing, but I can feel how much he loves it.) Talking to my sons and taking in their scent. Each of them has one spot on their heads where they still smell like the babies that I raised. I know right where to find the spot on each of them. It takes me back to the time when they were so small and vulnerable. But now they are grown men.

My sons are similar in so many ways and yet different. Both are studious and interested in fitness. Roland, my oldest son, and I have a lot in common. We are both extroverts, enjoy business, and tend to see life in a similar way. Derek and I are different, so we had to work more at our relationship. We struggled to get along during his teenage years, but now that he is and adult we seem to have found more common ground. The dynamics in our relationship changed completely once I accepted him for who he was. Unknowingly, I was trying to get him to see the world in the same way that I do. That led only to conflict. Basically, I was doing to him exactly what my parents did to me. I was showing him conditional love, and that is a recipe for failure.

SOME OF LIFE'S GREATEST PLEASURES ARE OFTEN OVERLOOKED WHEN WE ARE IN A PATTERN OF HIGH ACHIEVING.

I sit and watch the sunset. Smell a flower. I listen to my heartbeat and my breathing. All of this is important in life. Not just what you accomplish. Our world is fixated on accomplishments and motivation. During the COVID-19 pandemic, a motivational message circulated stating the following:

If you don't come out of this quarantine with either
A new skill
Starting what you've been putting off like a new business
Or more knowledge
You didn't ever lack the time; you lacked the discipline.

I am one of the most disciplined people I know, and yet I can admit that the state of the world during this pandemic had me feeling bipolar. I was almost certain I needed medication until I decided that whatever I was feeling was totally okay. If I was happy, great. Mad and cursing? Totally fine. Bitchy? Yup, okay in this situation. Sweet and sappy? New for me but also okay. I was productive, but not in the usual way, where I checked off each item on my to-do list. Instead, most days I only got a few things done and did what I needed to do to feel fine. Whether it meant exercising, enjoying nature, watching a stupid movie, or staring at the wall, I refused to judge myself. I didn't even judge myself when I drank wine most nights of the week or ate a whole box of Trader Joe's bon bons. I decided there may never be another situation where I could be alright with all these things so might as well take advantage of it!

It's fun to break all of those goddamn rules you live by. What rules, you ask? Well, we all have different ones, but mine go something like this...

- ✷ Workout six days a week
- ✷ Don't drink too much (no more than four drinks a week)
- ✷ Don't take a bite of that chocolatey delicious cereal your kids are eating
- ✷ Don't watch too much TV
- ✷ Wake up early every morning
- ✷ Get through my large to-do list
- ✷ Meditate, journal, stretch
- ✷ Check off each item on your to-do list unless you want to be a loser

Sometimes, though, you have to say "Fuck It" to your own damn rules and break them. That's where some real freedom arises. Freedom to make and break your own damn rules when the time is right.

I was hardwired to achieve starting in kindergarten. I learned how to achieve without living. I learned how to be cold and lock away all my emotions because emotions get in the way of accomplishments. Emotion was weak, and I wanted nothing but to be strong. Now I know I can have emotions, be strong, have boundaries, and ACCOMPLISH. These things aren't mutually exclusive.

Surrendering

I have never been one to succumb to fear, but as a Type A personality, I have always had a preconceived notion about how things should be. I have everything planned out. When things don't go according to my plans, I get stressed. According to Michael Singer, author of the *Untethered Soul,* stress is a byproduct of resistance. When we resist life's events due to fear or a preconceived notion about how things should be, this causes stress. Instead, if we comfortably handle the flow of our lives, we will not feel stress. As I reflect upon most of my life, I realize I have been resisting rather than accepting. I guess I have been trying to push back on the wave instead of just riding it. When you are riding the wave, you are in the flow. No resistance. If you fight it, it pushes you down, and you struggle for air.

Yup, that's what my life has been like.

I started to be an observer of my own life and noticed less and less was "happening to me." Therefore, I released the attachments. With time, it kept getting better. But it has taken me years to stop resisting and controlling. I controlled anything and everything I could. It was mentally and emotionally exhausting, so it had to stop.

Triggers

When I am being avoided, it triggers something in me. Something ugly. I would get mean and withdraw further.

I recently found out why this triggered and continues to trigger me in all my relationships. It stemmed from a childhood situation when I was four years old. My hair was combed with a small barrette neatly in place. I was in one of my nicest dresses, waiting…waiting…for my daddy to come home, scoop me up, and show me some affection. He usually came home somewhat late, but if he was really late, he would get me a delicious cookie from the subway. A freshly baked shortbread cookie with sprinkles on it as a peace offering for making me wait. It was 1973, way before text messages and cell phones, so we never knew what time he would arrive. I waited obediently in order to get rewarded. I didn't realize back then that somehow this would condition me for the rest of my life. How many women have been taught to wait patiently for a man to reward us?

My mother had to fight me for my dad's affection. On the weekends, I cleverly climbed into bed between them, pushed my mother out of the way, and in no uncertain terms demonstrated that he was in fact "MY DADDY!" Turns out Freud and Jung were onto something. Apparently, I had daddy issues I wasn't even aware of.

EPILOGUE

You know that exercise therapists ask you to do to find your authentic self? The one where you ask yourself who you are if you are on a deserted island without your loved ones, career, and material possessions? Well, life in isolation during a pandemic is the closest I might get to that. Everything is closed, so I can't get my Brazilian blowout or wax, can't get my nails done or my haircut. When I go out, it is only for essentials and not for pleasure. I go to work, but I don't have a full patient load, so I don't feel like the successful woman I have become accustomed to. I know I still have it good because I have a roof over my head, my children are within reach, and I have the comforts of my own bed. But somehow, I feel like I am a shell of the person I used to be. I wonder why that is, and it makes me think. It makes me think hard to find out why I am so uneasy every day.

Before isolation, my life was filled with a lot of people and noise. I didn't know how to be by myself for long periods of time. I often felt lonely. But something beautiful emerged from my isolation. I got to the point where I didn't need and strangely didn't want to see so many other people. There was less "noise." My head was clear and quiet. But I ached all over.

The ache came from the removal of each part of my persona I was attached to but forced to give up during this isolation. I was attached to my role as a doctor, and I hadn't been able to work at my full capacity. The role of entrepreneur was hard to feel because of all the other things going on in the world. I was attached to money, but after the stock market crash and a steep decline in my practice, I didn't have that to make me feel secure. I am and have always been attached to people. People I cannot see, be around, or touch during a pandemic. I am very attached to physical touch, but I barely want it because it is not worth the risk of COVID-19. It was clear that I needed these roles, touch, and material things to make me feel safe and secure, but every day I learned to let go a little more.

There is absolutely no rule book for life. Most of us are too busy wondering what the right way to live is instead of focusing on the right way for us. Some of us turn to religion, cults, celebrities, and other people looking for answers. Only we can know what our final destination is and how we need to live our lives to get there. The moment you start turning to others for direction, there must be a realization that you need to get grounded in yourself. If you allow them, others will only lead you astray. They will continually lead you away from yourself if you choose to follow. Undoubtedly, most of the people you ask for opinions are probably more lost than you are, unless they continually do self-work.

The future is always uncertain. I can't plan or orchestrate my best ending to this scenario. No one can. We are all forced to deal with the events of the world as they unfold daily. What I do know is that I am not bound to the role of being a doctor, wife, mother, or daughter. No matter what happens, I will be alright. I am the lotus. I rise from the mud.

I am beauty unbound.

ACKNOWLEDGMENTS

I want to thank:

My brother – For his guidance and enthusiasm in helping me pull *Beauty Unbound* out of my head and onto these pages. For helping me share my truth, and for being there for me since childhood without fail. For accepting me no matter what and always encouraging me to be my best, most unbound self.

My sons – For their love, loyalty, and steady support through both stormy seas and calm waters. For first seeing me as a human being with her own life and ambitions and then secondly as their mother. you are my life's greatest gifts, and I love and cherish every moment with each of you. My life is much richer with the honor of being your mother.

My bonus parents – To my bonus parents, who always supported me with strength and kindness even though we weren't related by blood, but we bonded with love. A relationship that is truly unbound from society's expectations.

To my parents – To my father, who had the courage to cross the ocean with $40 in his pocket and the vision of a better life for his family. To my mother, who raised and nurtured three children while putting all her dreams aside so she could be a mother. I am grateful for your love, your support and all the sacrifice you both made on my behalf.

TO BOOK DR. SUNDAR FOR A SPEAKING ENGAGEMENT, VISIT DRKALPANASUNDAR.COM

LINKED IN:
LINKEDIN.COM/IN/DRKALPANASUNDAR

INSTAGRAM:
@KALPANA.UNBOUND

PODCAST:
THEUNBOUNDPODCAST.COM

CPSIA information can be obtained
at www.ICGtesting.com
Printed in the USA
JSHW071659270523
42092JS00006B/4/J